THE GOSPEL COMES TO LIFE

LECTIO DIVINA WITH THE
SUNDAY GOSPEL READINGS

Be Alert!

THE GOSPEL COMES TO LIFE

LECTIO DIVINA WITH THE
SUNDAY GOSPEL READINGS

Be Alert!

YEAR B

(2024, 2027, 2030)

Kevin Saunders

Philadelphia

BE ALERT! LECTIO DIVINA FOR YEAR B (The Gospel Comes to Life)

Written by Kevin Saunders
Edited by Peter Edman

For more Bible resources, visit Bibles.com

In this series:
THE GOSPEL COMES TO LIFE
LECTIO DIVINA WITH THE SUNDAY GOSPEL READINGS

STAY AWAKE! (Matthew, Year A, 2023, 2026, 2029)
Paperback Print on Demand ISBN 978-1-58516-426-4 (Item 125537)
PDF Digital Download ISBN 978-1-58516-427-1 (Item 125538)

BE ALERT! (Mark, Year B, 2024, 2027, 2030)
Paperback Print on Demand ISBN 978-1-58516-428-8 (Item 125539)
PDF Digital Download ISBN 978-1-58516-429-5 (Item 125540)

BE VIGILANT! (Luke, Year C, 2025, 2028, 2031)
Paperback Print on Demand ISBN 978-1-58516-430-1 (Item 125541)
PDF Digital Download ISBN 978-1-58516-431-8 (Item 125542)

AMERICAN BIBLE SOCIETY
101 North Independence Mall East, FL8
Philadelphia, PA 19106

americanbible.org

Paperback POD: ISBN 978-1-58516-428-8 (Item 125539)
PDF Digital Download: ISBN 978-1-58516-429-5 (Item 125540)

CONTENTS

PREFACE

WELCOME to this encounter with the Scriptures. I am a Catholic Bible teacher who offers a course through the entire Bible, read aloud and commented upon by me, every chapter of every book over the course of a seven-year journey through the sacred text.

My love for and fascination with the Bible was enhanced during my course of study in Israel. I was blessed to serve the Hebrew University of Jerusalem (Mt. Scopus Campus) as the chaplain for the Christian students there. My position allowed me the opportunity to attend and participate in graduate-level courses on the Bible led by the preeminent scholars of the day. In these seminars I was introduced to the cultural world of the Middle East and how this worldview can reveal the deeper meaning of otherwise challenging texts.

How can the dead bury the dead? How can Jesus expect his disciples to hate their parents if they are going to love him? And how can a camel ever pass through the eye of a needle? These (and other) teachings of Jesus were meaningless to me until Jewish scholars at the university opened the door to the culture of Jesus and how that culture informs his teaching. My understanding of the Bible took off like a rocket from there.

In 2017, American Bible Society asked me to create a series of Lectio Divina reflections based on the Gospel readings for each Sunday in the liturgical calendar. I was thrilled with the invitation, not knowing where the opportunity might lead. Well, the result is *The Gospel Comes to Life,* a three-volume collection of my Lectio offerings for the three cycles of the Catholic Christian sequence of Sunday Gospel readings.

Four principles guide my reflections.

1. *The Bible is rooted in geography.* Understanding the geographic limits and features of the Middle East often guides insights into the Bible.
2. *The Bible emerges from history.* Real people, in real places, do real things that include their response to their culture and environment as well as to God.

3. *The Bible is informed by Middle Eastern culture and custom.* Honor and shame are two key cultural values that direct the narrative.
4. *The Bible is the Word of God,* whole and entire, and is God's final word to humanity.

The reader will note evidence of each of these four principles in my writing. I hope these Lectio reflections will inspire you to dive deeper into the Bible—and into the culture of the Middle East, for its customs reveal much of who Jesus was, is, and will forever be.

It has been a blessing and an honor to complete the reflections that you have in front of you. My prayer for you—as you read, meditate, pray, and apply the Gospel lessons to your life—is that you will grow in faith as much as I have done in creating each Lectio.

I am indebted to American Bible Society for offering me the opportunity to write these Lectios and to the staff who edited my musings week by week over three years. A writer is only as good as his editor and mine have been the best! It has been wonderful to work with ABS and I look forward to more fruitful engagements in the future. Until then, blessings!

KEVIN SAUNDERS
Phoenix, Arizona
March 2023

INTRODUCTION

Lectio Divina means "divine reading" in Latin. It is an approach to Bible reading that invites you to slow down and tune out the noise (from within and without) by inspiring and equipping you to sit in silence and listen for God's voice in Scripture. This way of reading and praying through Scripture has been practiced for centuries and is still exceptionally relevant for today's distracted culture. You can practice Lectio Divina by yourself or with a group. One Lectio exercise includes four (or sometimes five) steps and will usually take about fifteen or twenty minutes.

THE STEPS OF LECTIO DIVINA

Prepare your heart, making it available. Be ready to listen. Lower the tone of the voices around you. Ask the Holy Spirit to accompany and guide you to perceive God's voice that speaks through the Scriptures.

1. READING *(Lectio).* **What does the text say?**

   Read through the Bible passage—slowly. Read out loud if you are part of a group, and maybe even if you are by yourself. Consider the people speaking or acting in the passage. Reflect on the time, place, feelings, actions, and senses involved. Write down what you discover. Leave room for silence after you finish reading the passage.

2. MEDITATION *(Meditatio).* **What does the text say to you?**

   Read through the passage slowly again. Focus on what strikes you personally in the passage. Explore what God is trying to show you through Scripture. Connect the text to your life circumstances and struggles.

3. PRAYER *(Oratio).* **How do you respond to the text?**

   Now that God has spoken to you through the Bible passage, you can respond to God in prayer. You can ask for forgiveness, give thanks, recite a memorized prayer, or write in a journal. You can also read a psalm or another suitable Bible passage as your prayer.

4. CONTEMPLATION *(Contemplatio).* **What can God teach you in silence?**

Lectio Divina incorporates silence in all its steps, but this step focuses on silence with more intention. Allow yourself to be embraced by God's presence. Sit quietly to take it all in—and listen for God's voice.

5. ACTION *(Actio).* **How can you apply God's Word to everyday life?**

Consider how what you experienced through reading, meditation, prayer, and contemplation might compel you to live differently today. What new practices can you incorporate into your life? How can you live out this experience in your community and public roles? Now is the time to put what you've learned into concrete action.

ABOUT THIS COLLECTION

This collection adapts a four-step approach to Lectio Divina. Each week's exercise combines READING with what might be called a STUDY step *(Studio)* to help you think about what the Bible passage says. The *Contemplatio* often includes both CONTEMPLATION and ACTION steps.

These Lectio are written for use by people from all traditions, including those new to the Bible. The readings follow the three-year cycle of the Roman Catholic Sunday Lectionary (the Revised Common Lectionary is nearly the same). Dates and Sunday observances vary slightly each time a cycle returns. This volume includes Lectio Divina written over two cycles of Year B (2018, 2021, 2024, 2027, 2030).

The reflections were written to be sent by email during the week before a Sunday observance. We also note the other Bible passages assigned for that Sunday so that readers may prepare for worship.

Each volume begins with the First Sunday of Advent. The titles are taken from Jesus's words in the opening Gospel for each year: *Stay Awake!* (Matthew, Year A); *Be Alert!* (Mark, Year B); *Be Vigilant!* (Luke, Year C). Each volume concludes with the Solemnity of our Lord Jesus Christ, King of the Universe. We hope you find comfort for your soul and prompting for your life as you meet this loving King and hear his voice in these pages.

Be Alert!

FIRST SUNDAY OF ADVENT

BE ALERT!

MARK 13:33–37

> 33 "Be watchful! Be alert! You do not know when the time will come. 34 It
> is like a man traveling abroad. He leaves home and places his servants
> in charge, each with his work, and orders the gatekeeper to be on the
> watch. 35 Watch, therefore; you do not know when the lord of the house
> is coming, whether in the evening, or at midnight, or at cockcrow, or
> in the morning. 36 May he not come suddenly and find you sleeping.
> 37 What I say to you, I say to all: 'Watch!'"

Lectio

It is time to prepare for the first Sunday of Advent. Advent is a four-week time of preparation in advance of the twelve days of Christmas (those twelve days begin on Christmas Eve and conclude on the Feast of the Epiphany). Advent translates a Latin word that means "coming" or "visit." Jesus has already appeared—and he is coming again! In the next four weeks we will read and study Gospel passages that remind us of our need for and expectation of a Savior as we appreciate each of these Advents. The first was in Bethlehem's manger and the second will be when Jesus returns to judge the living and the dead.

Our Gospel reading for this week is taken from the end of a chapter where Mark presents an apocalyptic discourse of Jesus. Jesus has just revealed details about certain historical events that will precede the destruction of the temple. His disciples naturally want to know more. After the destruction of the temple—when not one stone will be left upon another (Mark 13:2)—when will the entire world end? Jesus's answer comes just before this week's reading. He tells his disciples that "of that day or hour, no one knows, neither the angels in heaven, nor the Son, but only the Father" (Mark 13:32). The sense here is that the disciples are not ready, nor will they ever be, to know the exact day, much less the hour when the final judgment will come. To date every prophet who has predicted the day and the time and the hour has been wrong—100 percent wrong, 100 percent of the time!

Jesus tells his disciples that the countdown to the end of all things will begin with the destruction of the temple. From that point forward they will be called to stay awake and remain alert. In fact, in these few verses Jesus tells his disciples to be alert and stay awake three times. This the only answer he is willing to give to those who want to know more about the end of time and the final judgment. Just be ready.

This advice works well in the Middle East. The culture here operates in a present tense, and Jesus has himself taught his disciples not worry about the future, for today has enough trouble of its own (Matthew 6:34). It is easy for the Middle Eastern person to live only in the present, but our ancestors in faith needed a gentle prodding to keep future consequences in mind too. This is what Jesus is calling his disciples to consider today: The end is coming. Don't become complacent. Be alert and be ready.

Beware! Keep Alert! You don't know when the time will come but it will, and when it does you need to be prepared. Be on the watch! Be on the job! The Master of the house is going to return! Jesus is encouraging a future-oriented perspective that would not be the norm in his time or culture. Don't go to sleep on me now! Be ready! The end will come, inevitably, and you don't want to be found asleep and miss the great event.

This is countercultural teaching. When we're thinking about the end of time, our normal cultural expectations won't get the job done.

Meditatio

You and I are men and women of faith who live in the cultural norms of the West. We are hopelessly (a telling phrase) future oriented—so much so that we sometimes attend seminars to teach us how to be present in the moment. We run frantically after future prospects that change at the speed of technology. Yesterday is discarded, forgotten, as we look to a future that we hope will make our lives better and more productive.

Ironically, one of our problems may be that we don't get enough sleep. We are awake too much, anticipating what we might miss. This is sometimes known as FOMO, Fear of Missing Out. It keeps us on our screens for fear that we might miss something important—life-changing—that will otherwise pass us by.

Our future-skewed cultural worldview makes appreciating this Gospel passage a challenge. We need to slow down, to learn how to live in the present, and allow "holy anticipation" to enter our lives. This is the gift of the Advent season. We will listen to Gospels of anticipation and preparation that will culminate in the celebration of Christmas. Waiting is good; holy waiting is better. Advent gives us permission to wait again, to live in the present and to truly appreciate the gift of Christmas in the manger at Bethlehem.

Oratio

This would be a good week to pray with King David in Psalm 57:7–11 (NRSV). Remember the call of the Gospel is to be ready, to be alert, and to stay awake. "*My heart is steadfast, O God, my heart is steadfast. I will sing and make melody. Awake, my soul! Awake, O harp and lyre! I will awake the dawn. I will give thanks to you, O Lord, among the peoples; I will sing praises to you among the nations. For your steadfast love is as high as the heavens; your faithfulness extends to the clouds. Be exalted, O God, above the heavens. Let your glory be over all the earth.*"

Contemplatio

How can we put our faith into action this week? We remember that from a biblical perspective "deeds" must express "creeds." This is why it is important to contemplate ways we can live out the Gospel that we hear at Mass. Our Lectio preparation helps us participate in living out our faith during the coming week.

One positive response to this teaching of Jesus might be to ask the Lord to help us stay awake and be alert to those who are in need of our love and service. People in real need are all around us. When you ask the Lord to show you those in need you will be amazed at what you will see. Be ready to act. Be ready to serve. Be ready to give.

In Jewish spirituality all are called to express their faith in three ways. First, one is required to pray (twice daily), to fast (once annually on Yom Kippur), and to give to almsworthy recipients as often as you find them.

In the Middle East when alms are given to an Arabic-speaking person the translated response of gratefulness is "you're welcome!" Wait a minute! What happened to "thanks"? I researched this response and discovered that the almsworthy recipient knows that a believer is bound by faith to give alms to all who ask. To meet this expectation God has to put almsworthy persons in your path. When you give alms to the needy a response of "you are welcome" is appropriate. Why? Because you should be thankful that an almsworthy person was present in front of you to receive your gift. "You're welcome," they say. "If I wasn't here you would have no one to give to, and you would not be able to fulfill the third part of your faith-life expectations." If we remain alert and awake I am sure we will find many occasions this week to bless others and in doing so will please our Father in heaven.

OTHER READINGS: ISAIAH 63:16b–17, 19b; 64:2–7; 1 CORINTHIANS 1:3–9

SECOND SUNDAY OF ADVENT

PREPARE THE WAY!

MARK 1:1–8

1 The beginning of the gospel of Jesus Christ the Son of God.

2 As it is written in Isaiah the prophet:

> "Behold, I am sending my messenger ahead of you;
> he will prepare your way.
> 3 A voice of one crying out in the desert:
> 'Prepare the way of the Lord,
> make straight his paths.'"

4 John [the] Baptist appeared in the desert proclaiming a baptism of
repentance for the forgiveness of sins. 5 People of the whole Judean
countryside and all the inhabitants of Jerusalem were going out to him
and were being baptized by him in the Jordan River as they acknowledged their sins. 6 John was clothed in camel's hair, with a leather belt

around his waist. He fed on locusts and wild honey. [7] And this is what he proclaimed: "One mightier than I is coming after me. I am not worthy to stoop and loosen the thongs of his sandals. [8] I have baptized you with water; he will baptize you with the holy Spirit."

Lectio

We are in the liturgical season of Advent, a time for prayerful expectation. Our reading this week is from the opening verses of Mark's Gospel. Our writer is drawing on the preaching of St. Peter in Rome, and as the Gospel begins he sets out a central element of Peter's teaching about Jesus. He opens with a bold, declarative statement that Jesus Christ is the Son of God, and the rest of his Gospel demonstrates that claim.

Jewish people in the time of Jesus were waiting for a Messiah (Hebrew for "anointed one"), sometimes referred to as the Son of David (Mark 12:35). They expected a Messiah from David's royal line to deliver Israel from the current occupation by the Romans. Mark makes a much bolder claim, a claim Jesus makes about himself: He is more than just a Son of David—he is the Son of God. This is an opening verse for the ages!

Mark starts by introducing a new character in his narrative, John. Who is this man who appears in the wilderness and starts preaching at the fording point along the Jordan River? Luke's Gospel identifies John as a cousin of Jesus born to his aging parents Zechariah and Elizabeth. He is older than Jesus by six months and the two cousins seem to know each other quite well. Perhaps they grew close over the years that the Holy Family traveled to Jerusalem to celebrate the pilgrimage feasts in Jerusalem. John stands in the waters of the Jordan and invites any and all to be dipped under the flowing current—but why?

All Jewish men and women must take a ritual bath before coming before the Lord to witness sacrificial offerings made on their behalf. This bathing is normally done in a "mikvah," a stepped pool that allows the worshiper access to a chamber of moving water. A river, the ocean, or even the Sea of Galilee can be used to the same end (the Sea of Galilee is created by the flow of the Jordan River through its basin). As long as the water is moving, the ritual bathing is valid.

What surprises me is that people are coming to John from Jerusalem. The residents of the city can bathe in one of the hundreds of "mikvahot" built near the temple complex for this very purpose. The Jordan River is a seventeen-mile trek, with a change in elevation of 3,500 feet—and then you have to go back! Nevertheless people are finding their way to John. This is unusual behavior and their pilgrimage draws the attention of the Jewish religious leaders.

John is described as dressing in a manner that evokes comparison with the prophet Elijah, who worked near this same fording point hundreds of years earlier. Before his famous chariot ride into heaven, Elijah parted the waters of the Jordan and passed through on dry ground (2 Kings 2:1–18). John's clothing recalls the prophet as well. It is coarse, woven from the belly hair of a camel—more like our burlap than anything else. His diet suits his work. Dried locusts are fried and dipped in spices for eating. The "wild honey" refers to processed fruit of the date palms that grow in the saline soils around Jericho and south to the Dead Sea. The dates would give him the energy needed to stand in the current and welcome men and women into the river where he would dip them under the water.

Many people were drawn to John and the Jordan, where they would confess their sins. They would engage in this ritual washing in advance of attending the Atonement sacrifice that was offered twice daily at the temple. After this ritual washing they were "clean" before God and so ready to receive God's forgiveness.

Meditatio

The baptism of John was not "for" the forgiveness of sin. The sins of a penitent were not washed away by this dipping gesture. Rather, submersion in moving waters prepared you to receive the forgiveness of sin that you desired as the priest offered a sacrifice on your behalf. It is more accurately translated that John dipped people under the waters of the Jordan "toward" the forgiveness of sin. We know that these men and women would go back to Jerusalem where they would be present near the temple for the atoning offering that would be made the next day.

In the Bible sin is described as a condition of alienation and separation from God. It can be evidenced by degree. Some sin is simple, some sin is more serious, and some sin is so significant that it will imperil your immortal soul. Unless confessed, sin cannot be properly diagnosed and its effect will always get bigger over time.

John is an agent of challenge and change. He is a strong man, living rough in the wilderness, who can stand all day in the Jordan's current and dip all who come. In Matthew 11:11, Jesus says that among all those born of women (and that includes the patriarchs), there has never risen anyone greater than John. That is high honor and praise for a cousin, a herald, and a friend. Women and men are irresistibly drawn to John because they feel the presence of God in his ministry. They travel miles out of their way to be dipped in these waters by him. Some even wonder if he could be the Messiah. Others honor him as yet another in a long line of great prophets. But he never honors himself and only points to the one who will come after him, the one whose sandal strap he is not worthy to untie. We would be hard pressed to find a more compelling figure in the time of Jesus and beyond.

Later John will say that he must decrease so that Jesus can increase (John 3:30). This is an excellent point of meditative reflection for you and me this week. We need to get out of the way so that Jesus can be revealed to others by the way we live and love as believers in the world.

Oratio

The Gospel theme of repentance recalls to my mind the great prayer of the penitent King David. This week we can pray with David in Psalm 51:6–12 (NRSV):

"You desire truth in the inward being; therefore teach me wisdom in my secret heart. Purge me with hyssop, and I shall be clean; wash me, and I shall be whiter than snow. Let me hear joy and gladness; let the bones that you have crushed rejoice. Hide your face from my sins, and blot out all my iniquities. Create in me a clean heart, O God, and put a new and right spirit within me … Restore to me the joy of your salvation, and sustain in me a willing spirit."

Contemplatio

How far would you go to find a John the Baptist in your life? What would it take to motivate you to come into contact with this kind of firebrand of faith? Thousands flock to him every week. He never seems to tire. He is God's man in the wilderness and even has a few choice words for the Jewish ruling class and King Herod. No time spent near him is without excitement.

Still, John remains a servant with a servant's heart. Given a chance to speak, perhaps in response to the accolades he receives from the crowds, he always states that he is not worthy of public praise. He is serving the one who is coming after him. He tells those at the shore that what they have experienced in the waters of the Jordan they will experience again when the Messiah comes and they are baptized in the Holy Spirit.

This is a good week to look for opportunities to serve. Find a sandal strap or two that you can untie. A symbolic foot that you can wash. A soul that you can refresh with a kind word or by paying careful consideration during a conversation. Be a witness like John this week. John can be bold, bloody, and resolute at times. But John is a servant at heart. Pray that you can find that same servant's heart this Advent season.

OTHER READINGS: ISAIAH 40:1–5, 9–11; 2 PETER 3:8–14

THIRD SUNDAY OF ADVENT

LET YOUR LIGHT SHINE!

JOHN 1:6–8, 19–28

[6] A man named John was sent from God. [7] He came for testimony, to
testify to the light, so that all might believe through him. [8] He was not
the light, but came to testify to the light.

[19] And this is the testimony of John. When the Jews from Jerusalem sent
priests and Levites [to him] to ask him, "Who are you?" [20] he admitted
and did not deny it, but admitted, "I am not the Messiah." [21] So they

asked him, "What are you then? Are you Elijah?" And he said, "I am not." "Are you the Prophet?" He answered, "No." [22] So they said to him, "Who are you, so we can give an answer to those who sent us? What do you have to say for yourself?" [23] He said:

"I am 'the voice of one crying out in the desert,
"Make straight the way of the Lord,"'

as Isaiah the prophet said." [24] Some Pharisees were also sent. [25] They asked him, "Why then do you baptize if you are not the Messiah or Elijah or the Prophet?" [26] John answered them, "I baptize with water; but there is one among you whom you do not recognize, [27] the one who is coming after me, whose sandal strap I am not worthy to untie." [28] This happened in Bethany across the Jordan, where John was baptizing.

Lectio

Preparing for the third Sunday of Advent, we find ourselves in the opening chapter (and prologue) of the Gospel according to John. We met John (called the Baptist in the Synoptic Gospels) in week one of Advent. This week we learn more about the man, this time from his testimony about himself. (Our Gospel author is, according to tradition, not this John but the apostle John, the youngest apostle and brother of the apostle James.)

We learn first that John the Baptist was a man sent from God, not as the Light that was to come into the world but rather as a witness to that Light—the herald who would announce the appearance of the Messiah to Israel. "The Light," a reference to Jesus as the Messiah, was coming into the world as Jesus would soon appear at the shoreline of the Jordan River to be baptized by John.

In this account John is challenged by two separate groups of religious leaders who send delegations from Jerusalem to determine if John considers himself the Messiah of God or not. The first delegation to arrive are priests and Levites who are sent from "the Jews." These "Jews" in the Gospel of John were the elites among the party of the Sadducees who administered the temple and its sacrificial system. Pilgrims were fording the Jordan River on their way to Jerusalem. News quickly spread that a charismatic prophet had appeared in the wilderness and people were also leaving Jerusalem to visit the Baptist at the water's edge. This delegation asks John who he is, or more specifically if he considers himself to be the Messiah. John answers with an emphatic No! "Who are you then?" They need an answer to report back to their superiors. Are you Elijah returned from heaven? Are you "the Prophet," the one promised by Moses that Jewish people believed would appear before the coming of the Messiah? Again John responds in the negative. Well then, who are you? What do you have to say about yourself? John responds by quoting Isaiah 40:3. He is a voice crying out in the wilderness to make straight the paths of the Lord. This work would be important if you were preparing to welcome a distinguished guest into your city or village. John is on the job.

The second delegation arrives, this one sent by the party of the people, the Pharisees. They learn from the first group that John does not identify himself as the Messiah or as Elijah or as the Prophet. Their initial question reveals their befuddlement. If you do not consider yourself the Messiah or Elijah or the Prophet, then why are you baptizing? What is the purpose of this symbolic dipping in the waters of the Jordan? And why are so many people leaving Jerusalem and coming here to you? They are confused and also have to report back to their leaders. John sends them away with specific knowledge that the Messiah is coming, and that when he appears not even John would be worthy to untie the thong of his sandal. The stage is set, anticipation builds, the game is afoot. Jesus is about to be revealed for the first time in the Gospel.

Meditatio

The opening verses of this week's passage recall the first word God speaks in the Genesis account of creation: "Light!" We translate that single word into a phrase, "let there be light," for the sake of narrative continuity, but in Hebrew the word is simply spoken and "Light!" comes into existence. That light was good and its effect was felt as the darkness of the abyss fled before it (Genesis 1:1–4).

Later in this Gospel Jesus proclaims himself the "light of the world" and declares that whoever follows him, "will never walk in darkness, but will have the light of life" (John 8:12). Jesus and the "light" of Genesis are one and the same. John knows this about Jesus and understands his role to testify and point people toward that light so that, as Messiah, Jesus can reveal to the world the kingdom of God.

John came to testify to the light. He was not the light. That light was coming into the world. We also are called to testify to that light. When we give our lives to Jesus and follow the light in the way that we live our lives, we become living demonstrations of the transformation that is possible when light enters our life and darkness is forced to flee. We are born again, symbolically leaving the darkness of the womb to enter the bright light of day. There is no going back, only forward, onward toward the light!

Oratio

This is a prayer that I gleaned in paraphrase from an Anglican youth ministry program. It captures our Gospel theme of light quite nicely:

Lord, help us to be people who bring light to all those around us. Even though we have had our light extinguished at times, rekindle it again, and help us never to be ones to snuff out the light of another. May we be light to the world, and as we let our light shine, may others see our light and praise our Father in heaven. Amen.

Contemplatio

In the Sermon on the Mount Jesus tells his disciples that they are going to be the light of the world. Jesus says that no one lights a lamp and then hides it under a bushel basket. You light a lamp to put it on a stand so that it can give light to all who are in the room. In the same way city on a hill cannot hide its light from all who pass by. Jesus wants us to let our "light shine before others, so that they may see your good works and give glory to your Father in heaven" (Matthew 5:14–16 NRSV).

There it is again—good works. The way we live in service to others is known to and honored by God. The light we bring into the world through our faith expressed in our actions, is real. It can dispel the darkness that would otherwise engulf the world. We are the resistance. We have to let our life shine so that the world knows where hope can be found.

Take a moment to look into the night sky this week. On a clear and dark night no one notices the great patches of darkness between the stars. They notice the points of light that we call stars. The stars and the light they give draw our attention and hold our gaze. That is what light can do. The light of our faith draws the attention of others and holds that attention so that we become living witnesses in the way we live as Christians.

May your light shine brightly during the final week of Advent.

OTHER READINGS: ISAIAH 61:1–2a, 10–11; 1 THESSALONIANS 5:16–24

FOURTH SUNDAY OF ADVENT

HOW CAN THIS BE?

LUKE 1:26–38

26 In the sixth month, the angel Gabriel was sent from God to a town
of Galilee called Nazareth, 27 to a virgin betrothed to a man named
Joseph, of the house of David, and the virgin's name was Mary. 28 And
coming to her, he said, "Hail, favored one! The Lord is with you." 29 But
she was greatly troubled at what was said and pondered what sort of
greeting this might be. 30 Then the angel said to her, "Do not be afraid,
Mary, for you have found favor with God. 31 Behold, you will conceive
in your womb and bear a son, and you shall name him Jesus. 32 He will
be great and will be called Son of the Most High, and the Lord God
will give him the throne of David his father, 33 and he will rule over
the house of Jacob forever, and of his kingdom there will be no end."
34 But Mary said to the angel, "How can this be, since I have no relations
with a man?" 35 And the angel said to her in reply, "The holy Spirit
will come upon you, and the power of the Most High will overshadow
you. Therefore the child to be born will be called holy, the Son of God.
36 And behold, Elizabeth, your relative, has also conceived a son in her
old age, and this is the sixth month for her who was called barren; 37 for
nothing will be impossible for God." 38 Mary said, "Behold, I am the
handmaid of the Lord. May it be done to me according to your word."
Then the angel departed from her.

The angel Gabriel sent by God to a young woman named Mary in Nazareth is the same Gabriel who had six months earlier been sent to the priest Zechariah in Jerusalem to announce that he and his wife Elizabeth would conceive a son who would become the herald of the Messiah. This same Gabriel appeared to the prophet Daniel in a vision (Daniel 9) to announce that the promised Messiah was going to come into the world at a date to be revealed through the prophet. It seems that Gabriel appears in the biblical narrative to deliver messages from God about Messiah and his coming.

Mary is alone when Gabriel approaches her. In her culture women—especially young women—are protected from strangers by residing deep inside the safe confines of the family home. In public they are protected from untoward advances by moving about in groups of other women, in the company of their husbands, brothers, or uncles, or by coursing through the markets with young children in tow. This Middle Eastern pattern of protection is breached as a figure startles Mary in her inner sanctum. She is afraid because she is suddenly in the presence of an uninvited male. Most probably, as an archangel, God's messenger would be clothed in military garb. At first glance he could have appeared to be a Roman soldier! This explains why Gabriel immediately follows up on his greeting to Mary by saying, "Do not be afraid!" He comforts her by telling her that all will be well and that the Lord is with her.

We are also shocked to learn that Gabriel speaks to Mary about conception and birth. Such conversations are private, usually only topics raised between women, and certainly never between an unmarried girl and a stranger. We are intrigued. Where is this conversation going to lead?

Mary will bear a son and is to name him Jesus. This would strike her as unusual because she is pledged to be married to a man named Joseph. In the Middle East the firstborn son bears the name of his father. Not in this case. In addition, the son to be born to her will be called "Son of the Most High." He will be "the Son of God." He will reign forever on the throne of his ancestor King David. Mary knows that her child is destined to be the long-awaited Messiah of Israel.

To attest to the truthfulness of this bold declaration, the angel reveals to Mary that her relative, old barren Elizabeth, is already pregnant and in her sixth month of gestation. Gabriel says that this fact should prove that nothing is impossible with God. Our author is subtly suggesting that if we knew how old Elizabeth really was and how long she had hoped to bring a child into the world, we too would be amazed at the news that she was now heavy with child.

The final response of Mary reveals her Middle Eastern view of the world. She responds to the angel with a simple "as you wish" that becomes "may it be done to me according to your word" in English translation. Mary does not understand how or when all of this will happen, but she responds with faith. The news about Elizabeth excites her, and Mary expresses her openness to be the vessel that will be used to bring Messiah into the world. "As you wish," says Mary. She is a servant of the Lord.

Meditatio

In answer to Mary's practical question—"how can this be"—the angel explains that for his word to her to be fulfilled the Holy Spirit will have to come upon her and the power of the Most High overshadow her. The result will be that the child born to her will be called the Son of God.

Gabriel uses terms from her culture to reveal to Mary the role that God as a Father will play in the conception and birth of her son. A Middle Eastern husband has two primary roles: to "empower" and to "protect" his wife. God will take on these marital responsibilities. The empowerment will come when the Holy Spirit comes to Mary. The power she will experience is the gift of life that will result in her pregnancy.

God will also protect Mary; the Holy Spirit will "overshadow" her so that she will be kept from danger and harm. Mary knows that the reference to "overshadowing" means that in the months leading up to the birth of her son God will be as present to her as he was in the tabernacle of Moses in the wilderness (Exodus 40:34–35). Mary is the new tabernacle of God. She said yes so that the Savior of the world can enter history through her. Mary is the new Eve. She is going to be the mother of the Messiah, and the Messiah will also be the Son of God.

Oratio

We should pray with Mary this week. We can use the same words that Mary used to honor God at the end of the Gospel portion this week. Pause for a moment so that you can make the prayer of Mary your own: "Here I am, the servant of the Lord; may it be done in me according to your word."

Contemplatio

Even in our own time young Jewish women wonder when Messiah will come, and who God will chose to be the vessel for his birth. They wonder if someday this blessing might be their own. Mary shared that same expectation when she learns from the angel that she has indeed been chosen.

This passage presents a series of reversals. In the Bible, reversals are meant to slow us down, to make us pause, so we can contemplate the deeper meanings behind the story. Contemplate Mary, chosen by God to bring Messiah into the world. Her culture is dominated by old men. She is young and voiceless in a world that reverences age and eloquence. She becomes the unexpected agent of God when she says yes and accepts God's plan of salvation along with all its many consequences.

Her *yes* meant many things. She will have to share her vision and visitation experience with her betrothed, Joseph. What would his response be? She will have to wait for signs in her own body that she is carrying a child. When would she know she was with child? She will have to find her way to Elizabeth to share her joy, but Elizabeth lives nearly one hundred miles to the south. How could she visit her kinswoman and when? Beyond all this, the child to be born will be called the Son of God? That name alone is blasphemy to the ears of religious leaders in her time. She is a young woman facing some serious challenges. Sit quietly with these considerations as we continue to anticipate the celebration of Christmas.

OTHER READINGS: 2 SAMUEL 7:1–5, 8b–12, 14a, 16; ROMANS 16:25–27

THE HOLY FAMILY

LUKE 2:22–40

22 When the days were completed for their purification according to the
law of Moses, they took him up to Jerusalem to present him to the Lord,
23 just as it is written in the law of the Lord, "Every male that opens the
womb shall be consecrated to the Lord," 24 and to offer the sacrifice of
"a pair of turtledoves or two young pigeons," in accordance with the
dictate in the law of the Lord.

25 Now there was a man in Jerusalem whose name was Simeon. This
man was righteous and devout, awaiting the consolation of Israel, and
the holy Spirit was upon him. 26 It had been revealed to him by the holy
Spirit that he should not see death before he had seen the Messiah of
the Lord. 27 He came in the Spirit into the temple; and when the parents
brought in the child Jesus to perform the custom of the law in regard
to him, 28 he took him into his arms and blessed God, saying:

29 "Now, Master, you may let your servant go
in peace, according to your word,
30 for my eyes have seen your salvation,
31 which you prepared in sight of all the peoples,
32 a light for revelation to the Gentiles,
and glory for your people Israel."

33 The child's father and mother were amazed at what was said about
him; 34 and Simeon blessed them and said to Mary his mother, "Behold,
this child is destined for the fall and rise of many in Israel, and to be a
sign that will be contradicted 35 (and you yourself a sword will pierce)
so that the thoughts of many hearts may be revealed." 36 There was
also a prophetess, Anna, the daughter of Phanuel, of the tribe of Asher.
She was advanced in years, having lived seven years with her husband
after her marriage, 37 and then as a widow until she was eighty-four.
She never left the temple, but worshiped night and day with fasting and

prayer. [38] And coming forward at that very time, she gave thanks to God and spoke about the child to all who were awaiting the redemption of Jerusalem.

[39] When they had fulfilled all the prescriptions of the law of the Lord, they returned to Galilee, to their own town of Nazareth. [40] The child grew and became strong, filled with wisdom; and the favor of God was upon him.

Lectio

This week we celebrate the Feast of the Holy Family and the Gospel reading honors Joseph and Mary as pious and devout parents of Jesus. The Gospel opens after the forty-day purification period the law prescribes after giving birth to a male child. During these forty days the mother and son simply bond with each other. The normal day-to-day duties of the new mother are taken over by other women in the family. This is a time of blessing for Mary and her child Jesus.

At the end of the purification period, Joseph and Mary leave Bethlehem and travel with the baby Jesus five miles north to Jerusalem and the temple, where they will present him before the Lord and offer a sacrifice in thanksgiving for the birth of their son. Leviticus 12:1–8 details the expectation for the offering, and the parents know that the preferred offering is a year-old lamb. Joseph and Mary are unable to afford this offering and produce two young pigeons instead. This alternate offering is also acceptable to the Lord.

Joseph and Mary had recently traveled to Bethlehem to be counted in the local census. Their stay in the village was extended due to the birth of Jesus. Any funds that they had put aside to cover travel costs from Nazareth to Bethlehem and back were certainly depleted by the delay caused by the birth of Jesus and the forty-day period of purification. They cannot afford a lamb, but Joseph and Mary intend to offer the most they can afford as a gesture of thanksgiving in the temple.

In the temple they meet two prophets who reveal a heightened sense of expectation that the Messiah was coming soon to Israel. It appears that both the prophet Simeon and the prophetess Anna were waiting for the parents of the future Messiah to bring him to the temple for the purification ritual. They each speak to Joseph and Mary about the child Jesus and who he is destined to be. Simeon conveys the warning that Jesus will be a sign of opposition, and that a sword will pierce the heart of Mary when her son as Messiah is rejected and scorned. Anna, a widow of advanced years and considered wise, takes the child in her arms and comforts the new parents with words of praise and blessing for all in the temple to hear. Simeon and Anna were looking forward to the redemption of Jerusalem and each recognizes the Messiah when they hold Jesus in their arms.

Meditatio

Joseph and Mary are surprised and amazed at what Simeon and Anna say about Jesus. They already know the all the details of the annunciation, conception, and birth of their son. The angel Gabriel had communicated with each of them. They had honored Gabriel's direction to name their child Jesus. They followed the Levitical law by having their son circumcised on the eighth day and presenting him to the Lord in the temple on the fortieth day after his birth. Still, when they meet these two prophets they are amazed and surprised.

What would it take to surprise and amaze us this Christmas season? We know the story and many of us have celebrated the holiday for the whole of our lives. Is there any way that God can speak to us this year that will set us on a new course and provide new insights from familiar texts? Are we open to being surprised and amazed by his word again?

God used these two prophets to speak to Joseph and Mary about Jesus. Each was old—"advanced in years." Age is honored in the Middle East and with age comes wisdom. You trust people with white hair. When they speak, you listen. When these two spoke about the child Jesus, his parents were swept up in the holiness of the moment.

These two prophets are wisdom figures in the nativity story. Who are the wisdom figures in your life? Where do you hear from them? Is their wisdom the result of experience or education?

The Holy Family will now return to Nazareth where Jesus will be raised. He will learn a great deal from his parents that will prepare him for his public ministry. The journey that begins with the presentation in the temple will end with his death on a cross. That will be the sword that will pierce the soul of his mother, who is sometimes called Our Lady of Sorrows. The prophets have spoken and their words come to pass. And so the story begins …

Oratio

The words of Simeon to Mary in this Gospel passage are used in the night prayer of the church. The prayer is called the Nunc Dimittis and is the concluding prayer of the service as the people prepare for the night's rest. Pray this prayer before you lay down to rest for the night.

"Lord, now you can dismiss your servant in peace, according to your word; for my eyes have seen your salvation, which you have prepared in the presence of all peoples, a light for revelation to the Gentiles and for the glory of your people Israel."

Contemplatio

We know that the Holy Family is devout. Joseph and Mary are dedicated to living their faith as the law requires. They come to the temple to dedicate Jesus to God and in doing so express their faith in action. What can we learn from their example? They made the effort to come to the temple and God met them there in the persons of the prophets. That is how God spoke to them, and that is how God can speak to you. The prophets in our lives are our pastors, who prepare a message each week for our edification. We pray for them that they will always live in the expectation that the kingdom of God will be revealed in the world. That's the genius of good religion—it reconnects us to God. We express our faith in our willingness to gather together. We pray and honor the Lord with the sacrifice of our time and our lives. God always has something to say if we are willing to listen with an open heart.

The message we receive can even come from an unexpected source. It could be the pastor one week and the woman who greets you at the church door the next. You won't know if you don't go. Sometimes faith is as simple as showing up and being open to hear the Word in any way and by any means that the Lord might use to get your attention.

Simeon speaks directly to Joseph and Mary about the responsibility they have to raise their child so that he will become a "light for revelation to the Gentiles and for the glory of your people Israel." Anna shares words of consolation and comfort about the infant Jesus and his role as Israel's redeemer. The words of both prophets amaze Joseph and Mary. They learn so much in such a short time. They were faithful to their religious obligation to bring an offering to the temple in thanksgiving for the birth of their son. In return they leave filled with insight and hope about who their son is destined to be as the Messiah.

OTHER READINGS: GENESIS 15:1–6; 21:1–3; HEBREWS 11:8, 11–12, 17–19

THE EPIPHANY OF THE LORD

THE HEAVENS DECLARE THE GLORY OF GOD

MATTHEW 2:1–12

1 When Jesus was born in Bethlehem of Judea, in the days of King Herod,
behold, magi from the east arrived in Jerusalem, 2 saying, "Where is the
newborn king of the Jews? We saw his star at its rising and have come
to do him homage." 3 When King Herod heard this, he was greatly
troubled, and all Jerusalem with him. 4 Assembling all the chief priests
and the scribes of the people, he inquired of them where the Messiah
was to be born. 5 They said to him, "In Bethlehem of Judea, for thus it
has been written through the prophet:

6 'And you, Bethlehem, land of Judah,
are by no means least among the rulers of Judah;
since from you shall come a ruler,
who is to shepherd my people Israel.'"

7 Then Herod called the magi secretly and ascertained from them the
time of the star's appearance. 8 He sent them to Bethlehem and said,
"Go and search diligently for the child. When you have found him,
bring me word, that I too may go and do him homage." 9 After their

audience with the king they set out. And behold, the star that they had
seen at its rising preceded them, until it came and stopped over the
place where the child was. [10] They were overjoyed at seeing the star,
[11] and on entering the house they saw the child with Mary his mother.
They prostrated themselves and did him homage. Then they opened
their treasures and offered him gifts of gold, frankincense, and myrrh.
[12] And having been warned in a dream not to return to Herod, they
departed for their country by another way.

Lectio

Wise men, magi, from the east arrive in Jerusalem, much to the shock of a Jewish king and the general population. Christians imagine the visitors to be three in number based on the three gifts brought to honor the newborn king, but this would not fully explain the "great troubling" of King Herod and his subjects.

The wise men, traveling in a caravan laden with goods that will fetch a high price in Egyptian markets, make a detour to Jerusalem to honor the birth of a new king. The despotic King Herod is concerned about anyone who might claim the right to his throne, itself gifted to him by the occupying empire of Rome. Herod is not knowledgeable enough about his own faith tradition to know where the promised Messiah will be born. He has to consult his high court officials for insight. He learns that he should direct his attention to Bethlehem, a small village five miles to the south of Jerusalem. Suspicions arise among the magi when Herod calls them "in secret" in an attempt to find out when their journey began. The Middle East is a public culture and events that happen behind closed doors leave you musing about possible intrigue.

The wise men traveled for months to arrive in Jerusalem. They read the heavens—which still declare the glory of God (Psalm 19:1)—to deduce from the planetary movements that something special has happened in Judea. They come to honor the birth of the newest king in Israel.

The gifts they offer are suitable for just such an occasion. Gold is the common currency of the time. Frankincense is an extremely valuable resin offered not only on Egyptian altars but also before the Lord in the

Holy of Holies. Myrrh (in the form of an anointing oil) is sought after in Egypt as part of the extensive burial customs.

Each gift is received by Mary and Joseph. They could not have been aware that Herod would have designs on their son's life. They could not have known that through the wise man God had just financed their future flight into Egypt where they will flee to avoid the wrath of the deadly king.

Meditatio

The prophet Isaiah (49:6) promises that the Messiah will be "… a light to the nations, so that my salvation may reach to the ends of the earth." The wise men from the east traveled over 1000 miles by the time they reach Jerusalem. These Gentiles responded in faith and came to the holy city. Upon arrival they found that the named Jewish king could not answer their questions about the Messiah or his birth. The Gentiles see the light and follow the star. The Jewish king is not able to comprehend the importance of the message writ large in the heavens.

The gifts of the magi are also worthy of meditation. The fathers of the early church saw in gold a message about the royal status of the Messiah. He was to be the true king of Israel. In frankincense they saw a symbol of his divine nature, since this was the incense used in the temple and symbolized prayer rising to the heavens and its courts. In myrrh, the ointment of death used in Egyptian burial customs, they saw the humanity of the Messiah. He was the anointed one, God's final Prophet, and he would remind us all that prophets die doing the work of God.

Priest (frankincense), Prophet (myrrh), King (gold) are all aspects of the Messiah revealed in the Gospel. How do these gifts speak to you in your walk with the Lord? When is he Priest, Prophet, King in your life?

Oratio

"The heavens declare the glory of God; the firmament proclaims the works of his hands. Day unto day pours forth speech; night unto night whispers knowledge." (Psalm 19:1–3)

Like the wise men of old, keep our eyes gazing into the heavens. Your creation spoke of you then and speaks of you now. Give us eyes to see and ears to hear so that our lives can be lived for your glory. Give us the courage we need to follow the star that will lead us closer to you in this season.

Contemplatio

Wise men from the east notice a light in the sky. It pierces the darkness. That light is a star that moves them to travel a great distance in search of its meaning. Light has that effect. Jesus said that a city set on a hill cannot be hidden, and that a lamp must be placed on a pedestal so that it can give light to everyone in the house. We are attracted to light—and Jesus says that we now are to be light for the world.

Wise men from the east follow the light of the star searching for meaning. That search required effort, sustained over the course of months until they finally arrive in Jerusalem. During the journey did they wonder? Did they question their motives? Did they consider giving up? I suspect so, but they proved themselves to be open, engaged, and persistent. God led them to their destination and they share their gifts with the Holy Family.

How are we like these wise men? How far out of our way are we willing to go to find the Lord? What is the light the Lord is using to call us closer to him this week? Persistence paid off with the magi and persistence will pay off in our lives as well. That will be our lesson from the wise men this week. Follow the light.

OTHER READINGS: ISAIAH 60:1–6; EPHESIANS 3:2–3a, 5–6

SECOND SUNDAY IN ORDINARY TIME

NAMES AND TITLES

JOHN 1:35–42

35 The next day John was there again with two of his disciples, 36 and as
he watched Jesus walk by, he said, "Behold, the Lamb of God." 37 The
two disciples heard what he said and followed Jesus. 38 Jesus turned
and saw them following him and said to them, "What are you looking for?" They said to him, "Rabbi" (which translated means Teacher),

"where are you staying?" [39] He said to them, "Come, and you will see."
So they went and saw where he was staying, and they stayed with him
that day. It was about four in the afternoon. [40] Andrew, the brother of
Simon Peter, was one of the two who heard John and followed Jesus.
[41] He first found his own brother Simon and told him, "We have found
the Messiah" (which is translated Anointed). [42] Then he brought him
to Jesus. Jesus looked at him and said, "You are Simon the son of John;
you will be called Cephas" (which is translated Peter).

Lectio

We return to the world of John the Baptist. In this Gospel passage we learn that John has disciples. A New Testament disciple is best understood as a student of a single teacher, a rabbi. John has gathered students—here, Andrew and another unnamed disciple—who have been with him, assisting him in his quasi-religious duties of dipping people in the Jordan River. People they have baptized are on their way to Jerusalem to offer sacrifices at the temple. John directs his disciples' attention to Jesus. He calls Jesus the "Lamb of God." The day before he had used the same title for Jesus and said that Jesus was the one who would take away the sin of the world.

Bishop Robert Barron calls this the use of "temple talk." John the Baptist is the son of a Jewish priest and is familiar with the work priests do in the temple. A year-old unblemished lamb was the preferred sacrificial offering for the forgiveness of sin. But John is not pleased with the work other priests are doing in the temple. He begins his wilderness baptism ministry in response to his displeasure with the temple leadership. Andrew and the other disciple are clearly in support of John as their rabbi.

John directs these two disciples to follow Jesus. Jesus notices them trailing after him and asks them what they are looking for. Calling Jesus Rabbi—a title reserved for students who want to honor their teacher—they say that they want to know where Jesus will be staying for the Sabbath. Jesus invites them to come and see. They follow Jesus for the rest of the day and arrive late in the afternoon in the village of Bethany. The timing of the journey implies that they travel from Jericho to Bethany on a Friday. It is late in the day and the sun is close to setting, so Jesus invites them to spend the Sabbath with his friends. They would spend the next twenty-four hours with Jesus. It would have been early Saturday evening before Andrew, released from Sabbath travel restrictions, finds his way to Jerusalem and locates his brother Simon. Andrew cannot wait to introduce him to Jesus.

Jesus is impressed by Simon. He may have been regaled over the Sabbath rest by Andrew's stories about his brother Simon and his particular character. Jesus seems to like Simon instantly, and he promptly gives him another name, a nickname. He will be called Cephas (a name that translates into English as Peter). Simon's new name is "The Rock." This endearing nickname will contribute to a strong bond of friendship and loyalty between Jesus and Simon. In the Middle Eastern world of the biblical narrative, when you are given a new name you are being invited into deeper intimacy and long-lasting relationship. This is certainly going to be true in the life of Simon Peter.

Meditatio

Titles. They appear three times in this reading and will used again by the end of this chapter of the Fourth Gospel. John the Baptist calls Jesus "the Lamb of God." This Lamb will one day "take away the sins of the world."

Andrew and the other disciple honor Jesus with the title "Rabbi," indicating to Jesus that they would like to be his disciples now. He accepts and welcomes them when he invites them to travel with him to Bethany.

Andrew finds his brother Simon in Jerusalem and tells him that he has found the "Messiah." Andrew believes Jesus is the Anointed One promised to Israel by the prophets.

"Lamb of God," "Rabbi," "Messiah." These are all wonderful titles for Jesus. Who is Jesus for you? What title would you use to introduce Jesus to someone you know, to someone you love? What did it take for you to meet Jesus? Who was the John the Baptist in your life of faith? Who was the person who pointed you to Jesus and said to go and follow him? Who was the Andrew in your life? Who found you and invited you to "come and see"? Meditate on these questions this week.

Oratio

We should always thank the Lord that we have been invited into relationship with him.

Lord, I thank you for your invitation to follow you. I thank you for the people you put in my life that directed me to you. Give me the courage to step out in faith and invite others into this same communion that I have with you now. I need grace to lead me and peace to guide my heart and mind. Provide this grace to me this week so that I might have courage to invite someone to "come and see."

Contemplatio

Andrew meets Jesus and is so excited by the encounter that he has to find his brother Simon so he can meet the Lord. Have you ever been so excited about your relationship with Jesus that you would find ways to bring others to meet him? Where would you bring them? To your church? To your fellowship group? To your Bible study? To your Christian outreach ministry? To your family? Who are the people in your life to whom you could introduce others so they would know they were going to meet Jesus?

This is our challenge this week—to find someone we can invite to "come and see" so they can encounter Jesus in a new and dynamic way. Be open and listen to the Lord. The direction will come and the invitation will follow. May God be with you.

OTHER READINGS: 1 SAMUEL 3:3b–10, 19; 1 CORINTHIANS 6:13c–15a, 17–20

THIRD SUNDAY IN ORDINARY TIME

AN INVITATION TO CHANGE

MARK 1:14–20

14 After John had been arrested, Jesus came to Galilee proclaiming the
gospel of God: 15 "This is the time of fulfillment. The kingdom of God
is at hand. Repent, and believe in the gospel."

[16] As he passed by the Sea of Galilee, he saw Simon and his brother
Andrew casting their nets into the sea; they were fishermen. [17] Jesus
said to them, "Come after me, and I will make you fishers of men."
[18] Then they abandoned their nets and followed him. [19] He walked
along a little farther and saw James, the son of Zebedee, and his brother
John. They too were in a boat mending their nets. [20] Then he called
them. So they left their father Zebedee in the boat along with the hired
men and followed him.

Lectio

When we read the Gospel each week we need to be aware of the context so we can better understand the biblical text. Our reading this week opens "after John [the Baptist] had been arrested." We find Jesus in Galilee after his own baptism by John and his subsequent forty-day sojourn in the wilderness of Judea. Jesus has moved north to Galilee to avoid confronting Herod, who has recently imprisoned John. As we follow our "backstory" thread, we note that Jesus has also made his way to Cana and a wedding celebration (John 2) before arriving at his home village of Nazareth (Luke 4). In Nazareth Jesus enters the local synagogue and preaches a sermon that results in his being driven out of his own home village.

We know that Jesus had traveled to Cana in the company of Peter and Andrew, who live and work in Capernaum (John 1). Is it possible that they had invited him to visit their family there? If Jesus and his mother had been driven out of Nazareth it is possible that they found their way to Capernaum and the home of Andrew and Peter. This seems to be the case as the Gospel opens this week. Finally, I think that we can comfortably conclude that by the time Jesus calls the four fishermen to follow him he has already known them for a couple of months, and that he is most probably the house guest of two of them, Peter and Andrew.

Our backstory is important because it helps us understand why these four fishermen would leave their successful commercial fishing business to follow Jesus, the healing, preaching, and teaching Rabbi from Nazareth. They must have known him long enough to trust him when he called them into his exclusive company. Jesus knew they were ready to respond.

These four disciples were commercial fishermen. They lived in Capernaum along the western shore of the Sea of Galilee. They plied the waters of the sea at night and would return in the morning to sort their catch and repair their nets. Ancient fishermen used "gill" nets to harvest fish from the Sea of Galilee. In the process of a night's fishing, the fine fibers that make the nets easy and effective to cast at night would tear as the fish thrashed about. Each morning their final routine was completed as the nets were mended—the knots were re-tied and the nets were tested by casting them on the water. Then the nets were stored on the boat, ready for use the following evening. Jesus calls Peter, Andrew, James, and John to follow him just after this task is completed.

Meditatio

"Repent, and believe in the good news." This phrase marks the initial proclamation of Jesus as he begins his public ministry in Galilee. "Good news" is the literal meaning of the word *gospel.* Jesus announces this gospel to all who are willing to turn around and listen. That is what the word repent means—to turn around and pay attention to what the speaker has to say.

Jesus knows that before you can believe in the good news of the gospel you have to "repent." In this reading, Jesus is challenging us to stop moving away from the kingdom of God that he is going to reveal to the world. He wants us to stop, to turn around, and then to come back to listen and live.

The word repent also carries a deeper spiritual meaning. The Greek word behind our English translation is *metanoia.* "Metanoia" literally means to "turn around your mind." It is a call to change the way you have been thinking and consider a new way of looking at your life. The call to repent is an invitation to change. To change in the way that we think and to change in the way that we live.

Four fisherman leave their nets and their gainful employment to follow Jesus. He had known them long enough to trust that they might leave all behind to follow him. They had spent enough time with Jesus to be ready to respond to the invitation to discipleship. They put their faith in Jesus into practice by their decision to become his followers that day. Will we be ready to respond to that same call? Today? This week? This year?

Cardinal Newman (1801–1890) wrote that "To live is change, and to be perfect is to have changed often." That is the call of the Gospel this week and the source of our meditation. Are we willing to repent, to change our way of thinking, as we deepen our commitment to Jesus in the Word?

Oratio

"For my thoughts are not your thoughts, nor are your ways my ways, says the LORD. For as the heavens are higher than the earth, so are my ways higher than your ways and my thoughts than your thoughts" (Isaiah 55:8–9 NRSV). *Lord, give us grace to put on your mind this week. May your thoughts be our thoughts and your ways ours as we do our best to live as your servants this week.*

Contemplatio

"Be transformed by the renewal of your mind" (Romans 12:2). That's one possible application of this call to repent. It is not enough to *desire* change. It's in the actual doing, the change itself, that we are transformed. We know, for example, that we should serve the poor. That is the first step. When we actually serve the poor our lives are transformed and we learn to think differently about the poor, poverty, oppression, and other insights. The "good news" of Jesus begins with service, leads to death, and is validated by the resurrection on the other side of the grave. That is the gospel way of life—and one we need to emulate if we want to grow in our faith.

OTHER READINGS: JONAH 3:1–5, 10; 1 CORINTHIANS 7:29–31

FOURTH SUNDAY IN ORDINARY TIME

AS ONE HAVING AUTHORITY

MARK 1:21–28

> 21 Then they came to Capernaum, and on the sabbath he entered the
> synagogue and taught. 22 The people were astonished at his teaching,
> for he taught them as one having authority and not as the scribes.

[23] In their synagogue was a man with an unclean spirit; [24] he cried
out, "What have you to do with us, Jesus of Nazareth? Have you come
to destroy us? I know who you are—the Holy One of God!" [25] Jesus
rebuked him and said, "Quiet! Come out of him!" [26] The unclean spirit
convulsed him and with a loud cry came out of him. [27] All were amazed
and asked one another, "What is this? A new teaching with authority.
He commands even the unclean spirits and they obey him." [28] His fame
spread everywhere throughout the whole region of Galilee.

Lectio

Capernaum is a well-populated commercial fishing village on the Sea of Galilee. As the Gospel opens this village is now the ministry headquarters of Jesus. We assume that Jesus lives in the home of Peter and Andrew and that he has become well known throughout the region since beginning his public ministry of healing, preaching, and teaching. The Gospels note that Jesus taught in synagogues across Galilee. The Capernaum synagogue would have been the home synagogue of Peter and Andrew, and also of James and John, the first four called into discipleship by Jesus. People are aware of his reputation as he begins to speak that Saturday morning.

The Jews are careful to ensure that all can understand the meaning of their Scriptures. Saturday morning in the synagogue is a time for communal education. People gather to hear readings from the Scriptures and listen to commentary by those who read. The last person to read a Bible portion would be welcome to comment on any of the other texts that had already been read, in addition to the one he had just completed.

Jesus is an expert teacher. He teaches with authority. He does not teach like the scribes, a class of Levitical priests who studied the Torah, transcribed it from scroll to scroll, and wrote commentaries about it. Scribes were highly respected, the Bible scholars of their time. Jesus knows this class of scholars well, and in the Sermon on the Mount he challenges his disciples to exceed the righteousness of the scribes if they want to enter the kingdom of Heaven (Matthew 5:20). By his time, the scribes had become a professional class of Bible teachers who had lost their passion for preaching the Word of God.

Suddenly, unclean (or evil) spirits are stirred to act. A man cries out in a voice not his own. He boldly claims that he knows who Jesus is, that his Father is God, and that he comes to them from Nazareth. The spirit is trying to control Jesus with this authoritative pronouncement. If you know someone's name and use it in this manner you may have power over the individual—like a parent today might use the middle name of a child when issuing directions. Jessica becomes Jessica Clare and Kevin becomes Kevin Dean, to emphasize that the parent has more authority than the child who was named at birth.

Jesus knows this is a challenge and immediately issues a stern command for silence. He orders the malevolent spirit out of the man. The unclean spirit obeys in an instant! A shocked calm follows. Who is this man Jesus? All present are amazed at Jesus's authority over the unclean spirits and in his ability to teach the Bible like they have never heard before.

Meditatio

In the synagogue in Capernaum those attending that day "were astounded at his teaching, for he taught them as one having authority." There was real power in the way that Jesus read and commented on the sacred text. The Word of God in the scroll came alive in a way that they had never experienced before. Then suddenly that awful cry, a voice from beyond this world challenges Jesus as the Rabbi that day. The voice of that unclean spirit tries to control Jesus by using his name and fails. Jesus silences the outcry and calm is restored.

The name of Jesus is powerful. The demon thought it could control Jesus by the use of his name. St. Paul knew better. He writes in Philippians 2:9–11 that God, "bestowed on him the name that is above every name, that at the name of Jesus every knee should bend, of those in heaven and on earth and under the earth, and every tongue confess that Jesus Christ is Lord, to the glory of God the Father."

That unclean spirit did bend to Jesus. It cried out and left the man healed before them all. A moment of silent amazement must have followed. Close your eyes and take a moment to imagine yourself in that synagogue that day.

We still call on the name of Jesus. When we do we tap into the power that created the universe. Jesus was in control that day and he is in control now. Call on the name of Jesus and know his saving love.

Oratio

Verses in Psalm 119 capture the power of the Word of God. We can use them in our prayer response to this Gospel passage.

"*How sweet are your words to my taste, sweeter than honey to my mouth! Through your precepts I get understanding; therefore I hate every false way. Your word is a lamp to my feet and a light to my path*" (Psalm 119:103–105 NRSV).

Contemplatio

Putting our faith into action is the goal of the contemplative life. We study, meditate, and pray to better hear God in the Word. Our next task is to incorporate what we have learned into the lives we live in service to others. The name of Jesus and the fame associated with his authority is beginning to spread far and wide in Galilee. The grapevine is working and the honor-status of Jesus is growing by the hour. That honor will be challenged, publicly. It always is. But Jesus is prepared for the test, every time.

Our faith will be tested too. It will be challenged by others. We have to be ready when the challenge comes. Our study and prayerful meditation on the Word of God will prepare us to pass each test. When we act in faith God's goodness is revealed to the world. There will always be those who push back, those who cry out and want to silence our witness. We need to be strong and confident in Jesus and in the power of his name.

OTHER READINGS: DEUTERONOMY 18:15–20; 1 CORINTHIANS 7:32–35

FIFTH SUNDAY IN ORDINARY TIME

EVERYONE IS LOOKING FOR YOU

MARK 1:29–39

29 On leaving the synagogue he entered the house of Simon and Andrew
with James and John. 30 Simon's mother-in-law lay sick with a fever.
They immediately told him about her. 31 He approached, grasped her
hand, and helped her up. Then the fever left her and she waited on them.

32 When it was evening, after sunset, they brought to him all who were
ill or possessed by demons. 33 The whole town was gathered at the door.
34 He cured many who were sick with various diseases, and he drove out
many demons, not permitting them to speak because they knew him.

35 Rising very early before dawn, he left and went off to a deserted place,
where he prayed. 36 Simon and those who were with him pursued him
37 and on finding him said, "Everyone is looking for you." 38 He told
them, "Let us go on to the nearby villages that I may preach there also.
For this purpose have I come." 39 So he went into their synagogues,
preaching and driving out demons throughout the whole of Galilee.

Lectio

Our Gospel opens as Jesus leaves the synagogue of his Capernaum ministry headquarters after the Saturday morning gathering. He is on his way to Peter and Andrew's home. There Jesus and his growing band of disciples will gather for a meal. This lunch would have been prepared the previous afternoon (the Friday before that Sabbath). Anticipation runs high. Jesus has already preached a message unlike any they heard before and cast out demons from a man possessed.

When they arrive at the house Jesus is informed that Peter's mother-in-law is ill. Jesus enters and is invited to attend to the woman in one of the inner rooms where she is suffering from the ravages of a high fever. The fact that Jesus is afforded such intimate contact with her suggests that he has become a recognized and respected member of the family. Strangers would not have any such access to someone bedridden with illness. In Matthew 8:8 a Roman centurion in the same town does not expect Jesus to follow him into his home to heal a beloved servant. He famously tells Jesus that he need only say the word and his servant will be healed. In our Gospel Jesus is welcome into the inner sanctum of Peter's home.

The fact that Peter has a mother-in-law reveals that he is a married man. St. Paul reminds the Corinthians that the apostle Cephas (Peter) travels with a believing wife (1 Corinthians 9:5). Peter took his wife's mother into his home because she was a widow and had no living son to provide for her in her old age. She has found her place in the household. It appears that she is a good cook and is the person responsible for the prepared lunch consumed that very day.

The mother-in-law suffers from a high fever, perhaps the onset of malaria. Malarial infection was quite common in Galilee during the biblical era—and later. Just north of the Sea of Galilee lay a vast inland swamp where mosquitoes bred. This same swamp was finally drained in the 1950s with the intent of eradicating the malarial infestation in Galilee. As Jesus pulls her up by the hand, the fever leaves her. She rises to serve, and resumes the loving duties that give her life meaning.

After the sun sets a new Jewish day begins. Travel restrictions associated with the Sabbath are lifted. Commerce resumes and people move about freely. Many make their way to Jesus and the home of Simon, bringing with them the sick, injured, and others challenged by evil spirits. He heals them all. He silences the demons. Jesus does not want their acclaim. He displays great authority over all that evening.

Jesus heals deep into the night and then rests. Then, rising before others in the morning, he departs the village to find "a deserted place" to pray. He knows that no one will follow him, for this is the place he had been casting demons *to* the night before. In the morning, after the sun rises and it safe to go in search of Jesus, Peter and some others (there is safety in numbers) find Jesus in this deserted place and excitedly inform him that "everyone is looking for you." This is good news. The word has gotten out. It is time to expand the mission from Capernaum to the other towns and villages in Galilee.

Meditatio

"Everyone is looking for you." Peter speaks these words to Jesus when he finds him in that deserted place. What was everyone looking for? What message was Peter intending to convey? "Everyone is looking for you." Peter wants Jesus to know that many more have a need for healing themselves or harbor a desire to see healing come to someone that they know, someone they love. "Everyone is looking for you" means that when Peter finds Jesus, his intent is to bring others to witness his healing, delight in his preaching, and listen in awe to his authoritative teaching of God's Word.

That is how the message of the Gospel spreads, by word of mouth. Someone finds Jesus and tells another about the discovery. That person is invited to come and see for themselves. There is an authenticity in the invitation. We have seen and we believe and so we are compelled to tell others about the experience.

Have you ever had an experience of Jesus that was so profound that you had to share it with others? An experience of Jesus so powerful that you had to find someone and bring them to see for themselves that what you experienced is true? If you haven't, pray that you will.

Oratio

Lord, like the mother-in-law of Peter, heal me and restore in me a desire to serve. My sin can be an illness that, like a fever, limits my ability and taps my strength. I pray that, healed, I will be freed from my bondage and rise to be your witness in the world.

Contemplatio

We need to consider our call to action this week. We could take our cue from the response of Peter's mother-in-law. She lay ill in her bed with a high fever. She met Jesus and was healed. She rose quickly and began to serve others in the household. Or our response might be like that of the people in Capernaum who waited until sunset (the first available opportunity) and then brought their loved ones to Jesus for healing. Who do you know who needs to be prayed for that you can bring to the Lord? Ours might also be the response of Peter in the morning. He needed to find Jesus. Have we ever been that excited to find Jesus with the dawn of a new day? Where do you look for Jesus? In what "deserted" place have you found him before? Do any of these examples stir you to action? How will you respond to the Gospel this week?

OTHER READINGS: JOB 7:1–4, 6–7; 1 CORINTHIANS 9:16–19, 22–23

SIXTH SUNDAY IN ORDINARY TIME

HE STRETCHED OUT HIS HAND

MARK 1:40–45

> 40 A leper came to him [and kneeling down] begged him and said, "If
> you wish, you can make me clean." 41 Moved with pity, he stretched out
> his hand, touched him, and said to him, "I do will it. Be made clean."
> 42 The leprosy left him immediately, and he was made clean. 43 Then,
> warning him sternly, he dismissed him at once. 44 Then he said to him,
> "See that you tell no one anything, but go, show yourself to the priest
> and offer for your cleansing what Moses prescribed; that will be proof
> for them." 45 The man went away and began to publicize the whole
> matter. He spread the report abroad so that it was impossible for Jesus
> to enter a town openly. He remained outside in deserted places, and
> people kept coming to him from everywhere.

Lectio

The narrative context of this Gospel is informative this week. We begin by looking at the opening verses of the parallel story in Matthew 8, where we find that this healing is set immediately after Jesus concludes the teaching we call the Sermon on the Mount. Jesus is moving away from the natural amphitheater toward the road, in clear view of the hundreds who heard the Master Teacher at his best. As the crowds watch, Jesus is approached by a leper, a religious and social outcast, who falls at his feet to impede his progress. The leper cries out in faith. If Jesus wants to, he can heal him and restore him to his family and village.

The man's medical condition is described as leprosy in English translations. Medical experts tell us that the condition now known as Hansen's disease did not exist in the world of the Bible. The man does suffer from some outwardly manifested skin condition, perhaps something like psoriasis. His condition has been diagnosed as incurable by a priest who would have worked through all the applicable protocols from Leviticus 13. He would have been quarantined not once but twice, and still the skin condition lingered. He has been forced to live as an outcast with others with a similar condition (see Luke 17:11–14) and is also required to announce his presence by wearing a bell and shouting "unclean" as he approaches people in public. This man was not among the crowd that day but had listened to Jesus from a distance. He was convinced that he heard the words of God's prophet. Could Jesus be the Messiah that many were expecting to appear in Galilee? There was only one way to find out.

The man comes to Jesus and pleads for healing. Before Jesus pronounces him clean he touches the man. That loving gesture of touch speaks volumes about Jesus, the compassionate healer. Jesus only had to speak the words and the man would have been cleansed. Touch was not required—and it was even forbidden by law and custom. After his loving physical contact with the leper, Jesus speaks with the authority of the divine and the man is instantly healed! Jesus orders the man to show himself to the priest, the very same priest who had originally examined him and had placed him among the class of other lepers. That specific priest would subject him to a cleansing ritual that would assure the priest and the community that the leper was truly healed and that he was to be received back by his community.

Read the details prescribed for the restoration of a leper in Leviticus 14:1–17. The first part of this ritual involves two live birds, a bowl of water, cedar wood, hyssop, and scarlet yarn. One bird is sacrificed, and the other bird is set free, symbolizing the man's authentic healing. Later, lambs are slaughtered, and their blood—and after that, sacred oil—is applied to the former leper's right earlobe, right thumb, and right big toe. We understand that the healed person is to spend the rest of his life listening to the Word of God and also to use his hands and feet in God's service. These are rituals the man will never forget—nor will the priests. This is how his healing will be a witness to them. They too would have to consider if the Messiah might be in their midst.

Hundreds have witnessed the unexpected contact and dramatic healing that occurs between Jesus and this social outcast. The story will be told and told again so that the fame of Jesus increases and the local towns cannot contain the numbers who are flocking to him from every direction. The public ministry of Jesus has officially begun.

Meditatio

"Moved with pity, he stretched out his hand, [and] touched him ..." This is the action we will meditate on this week. Jesus is the Virgin-born, sinless, Son of God who can heal anyone with a single word. This man comes for healing and rather than speaking that healing word Jesus reaches out and touches the man. Why? What is Jesus trying to teach his disciples with this intimate gesture? This man is a social outcast, ostracized from family and friends—a man who has become identified as a walking disease rather than as a human being. He has not been touched by another human since the time of his final diagnosis. He has been alone in the midst of the community that comprised his former way of life. Jesus wants to address the human need to be embraced, to be touched, and to be cared for before he utters the words of healing, "Be made clean!"

We should hear a collective gasp from the crowd surrounding Jesus as he reaches toward the leper. If Jesus touches him, then Jesus too will be unclean. Why would Jesus subject himself to defilement? What lesson is he trying to convey? That should keep us in meditation for a few moments today. Do we need such a touch ourselves? Who are the lepers in our culture? Who are those who are in need of our human touch and compassion?

Oratio

Our prayer this week is the prayer of the leper in the Gospel as he kneels before Jesus. He honors Jesus as a healing agent of God and expresses his faith in Jesus as he cries out, "If you choose, you can make me clean." That is a statement of biblical faith that should inspire us all. "Jesus. I come to you. I am in need of healing. If you choose, you can make me clean!"

Contemplatio

What lepers in your life do you feel the call to reach out and touch this week? Who is in need of healing? Lost friends? Out-of-touch siblings? Forgotten parents? The homeless? Persons of a different ethnicity? Fans of the other team? Who would you normally never touch or even speak to in the normal course of your day? Why? What keeps you apart? What can you do to cross the divide? What can you do to break through and reestablish communication, bringing healing in its wake? You are empowered by the Holy Spirit. If you choose, you can bring healing into your world.

OTHER READINGS: LEVITICUS 13:1–2, 44–46; 1 CORINTHIANS 10:31—11:1

FIRST SUNDAY IN LENT

THE ANGELS WAITED ON HIM

MARK 1:12–15

> 12 At once the Spirit drove him out into the desert, 13 and he remained in
> the desert for forty days, tempted by Satan. He was among wild beasts,
> and the angels ministered to him.
>
> 14 After John had been arrested, Jesus came to Galilee proclaiming the
> gospel of God: 15 "This is the time of fulfillment. The kingdom of God
> is at hand. Repent, and believe in the gospel."

Lectio

We return to the first chapter of Mark as we enter the season of Lent. The author is recording the preaching of St. Peter and has collected the memories of the apostle in this, the shortest of the four Gospels. It has opened powerfully with the announcement that it is the beginning of the good news of Jesus Christ, the Son of God. Mark does not pull any punches. He gets right to the point with a bold twofold claim about Jesus. He is the expected Messiah and the Son of God. How will the reader respond? That is the challenge for you and me this Lent.

This week's passage follows the baptism of Jesus in the coursing waters of the Jordan River. At the conclusion of the baptism, a voice from Heaven—God's voice—announces that Jesus is God's beloved Son and that God is pleased with him. This would be recognized as a public claim to honor that must be challenged by someone if it is to be proven true. This is how the honor- and shame-based culture of the Middle East operates. Any public claim to honor will be challenged in public before it is verified and believed. Events follow that reveal Jesus's ability to verify the claim made about him by his Father.

Jesus is driven out into the wilderness where he will face forty days of temptation by his enemy, Satan. Jesus bests the tempter. We also learn that Jesus was cared for by God's angels. Mark omits details of the temptations, but we learn about them in the Gospels of Matthew and Luke. All three synoptic authors agree that Jesus is the victor in this spiritual exchange.

After his victory over Satan Jesus returns to the baptismal site where he learns that John the Baptist has been arrested and is in prison. Perhaps concerned that he might found guilty by association Jesus gathers a new and growing group of disciples (see John chapter 1) and leaves the area around Jericho and heads north to Galilee. In Galilee Jesus will begin his public ministry. Over the next three years he will spend nearly eighty percent of his time in that region.

In Galilee Jesus proclaims boldly that "The time is fulfilled, and the kingdom of God has come near; repent, and believe in the good news" (NRSV). What does Jesus mean when he refers to the kingdom of God coming near? He is probably referring to a prophecy found in Daniel 2:36–45, where the prophet Daniel predicts the rise and fall of four kingdoms before the appearance of the one final kingdom of God that will stand for all time. A traditional interpretation of this passage is that the first empire to rise and fall is Babylon, the second is the Medo-Persian Empire. Then the Greeks come and go and are replaced by Rome's worldwide domination. In its turn, Rome will be crushed by a new kingdom, a kingdom built upon a stone that is cut out of a mountain, but not by human hands. It will bring the fourth kingdom to its end and will fill the whole earth (Daniel 2:35, 44–45).

Jesus calls on the people in Galilee to repent. He wants them to turn around and come to him. Jesus presents the possibility that the prophecy of Daniel is going to come to pass in their lifetime! The only way to know will be to listen to the one they know now as Jesus of Nazareth. And so his public ministry begins.

Meditatio

"[A]nd the angels ministered to him." This narrative detail of angelic comforters ministering to Jesus is compelling. Why does Mark include it in his concise mention of Jesus's forty days in the wilderness tempted by Satan? This aspect of the Gospel is worthy of our meditation this week.

In the Mediterranean world of our ancestors in faith everyone is connected to a kindred group. Everyone is connected to a family, to a clan, and to a tribe. You are loyal to that group and are constantly surrounded by them. They know you. They love you. They will protect you. There are no "Lone Rangers" in the New Testament era. In the account of the temptation Jesus is driven into the wilderness by the Spirit of God. He is alone, vulnerable, and open to attack by any and all who might find him. As a reader, we should ponder some questions this raises: Who will care for him? Who will watch over him? Who will protect him?

God will and God does. Jesus has been introduced to us in the first verse of this Gospel as the Christ and as the Son of God. The angels of God are of his family. They are there to make sure he is cared for during his time of testing. This information comforts the Middle Eastern person of faith. Jesus is never alone, even when he is in the wilderness facing his greatest adversary. Angels minister to him and we can ask our Father to send them to minister to us as well. This is one of the ways we can know that we are never alone.

Oratio

I memorized this prayer to my guardian angel as a young boy. It has served me well over the years and I will share it with you. It will ring familiar in Catholic ears: "*Angel of God, my Guardian dear, to whom His love commits me here, ever this day and night be at my side, to light and guard, to rule and guide. Amen.*"

Contemplatio

In the New Testament the word "repent" means to turn around and come back to where you were, to return to the source. "Repent" will be our call to action on this first Sunday in Lent. When Jesus calls people to repent he is inviting us to come back to him, to listen to what he has to say, and to see what he is doing in our world.

What are you called to come back to this Lent? What will your spiritual practice consist of during this season? Is it time to come back to one or more spiritual practices from your youth? Take a few moments in prayer and ask the Lord to show you what he has waiting for you. What awaits when you return to church? When you return to your extended family? When you reach out in an effort to restore a broken relationship? When you recommit yourself to meeting the Lord in the Word and in your daily prayer? The list goes on and on. It's time to repent this Lent and return to the Lord and the blessings God has in store for us these next forty days.

OTHER READINGS: GENESIS 9:8–15; 1 PETER 3:18–22

SECOND SUNDAY OF LENT

THE MOUNTAINTOP

MARK 9:2–10

2 After six days Jesus took Peter, James, and John and led them up a
high mountain apart by themselves. And he was transfigured before
them, 3 and his clothes became dazzling white, such as no fuller on
earth could bleach them. 4 Then Elijah appeared to them along with
Moses, and they were conversing with Jesus. 5 Then Peter said to Jesus
in reply, "Rabbi, it is good that we are here! Let us make three tents:
one for you, one for Moses, and one for Elijah." 6 He hardly knew what
to say, they were so terrified. 7 Then a cloud came, casting a shadow
over them; then from the cloud came a voice, "This is my beloved Son.

Listen to him." [8] Suddenly, looking around, they no longer saw anyone
but Jesus alone with them.

[9] As they were coming down from the mountain, he charged them not
to relate what they had seen to anyone, except when the Son of Man
had risen from the dead. [10] So they kept the matter to themselves, questioning what rising from the dead meant.

Lectio

Jesus and his disciples have been staying in Caesarea Philippi. Six days after arriving there Jesus takes his three trusted disciples—Peter, James, and John—on a journey that will find them on the slopes of Mt. Hermon, a mountain that overshadows Caesarea Philippi rising nearly nine thousand feet high in the distance. Somewhere along that journey they stop and gaze in wonder at Jesus who has been "transfigured" before their eyes. Mark describes the garment Jesus is wearing—suddenly it is whiter than any garment they had ever seen, more dazzling than anyone with bleach could achieve at that time. This insight would be useful to Mark's Rome-based audience, who would have been familiar with the Roman senatorial class and the gleaming white garments they wore to signify their office. Jesus is transfigured in a way that begged description in the normal world.

Then the disciples note the appearance of Elijah and Moses. They are speaking to Jesus. St. Luke notes that they were speaking about his "exodus" or the way that he would leave Jerusalem (Luke 9:31). For a Jewish person of faith Elijah and Moses represent the entirety of the Old Testament. Moses is the narrative author of the Torah, the first five books of the Bible. Elijah represents the rest of the Old Testament authors, who were all called prophets because they listened to God and spoke the words of the Lord to the people. Elijah is the prophet supreme—he did not have to suffer death but was assumed into Heaven, riding in a fiery chariot sent for him by God! These two biblical giants are speaking with the glorified Jesus and the three disciples are privileged to witness the event.

Peter speaks boldly on behalf of the three and suggests that they begin constructing booths, tent-like structures, one for Jesus and another two for Moses and Elijah. What was Peter's motivation for this suggestion?

It might be a reference to the prophet Zechariah. In Zechariah 14 the prophet speaks of the final judgment and the coming Day of the Lord. When the judgment is complete and God has revealed his saving power to Israel then the survivors from the nations will all travel to Jerusalem and celebrate the festival of Booths (Zechariah 14:16). Peter believes that with the transfigured Jesus this prophecy has come to fulfillment. Jesus is revealing himself as the divine Messiah on the mountain.

But Peter may be getting ahead of himself. God intervenes in the story. A cloud overshadows them, and from inside it God informs the apostles that they are to listen to Jesus, the Son of God. They need to heed his plan moving forward, a plan that will require a journey to Jerusalem where Jesus will have to suffer and die before being called back from the grave. That is the path they have to follow. This is not the time to construct the booths to celebrate the final victory over sin and death. That time will come, but it is not now. Coming off the mountain, Jesus swears them to secrecy until after he has risen from the dead.

Meditatio

"As they were coming down the mountain, he ordered them to tell no one about what they had seen, until after the Son of Man had risen from the dead" (verse 9, NRSV).

What is it about a mountain? Why do we climb to the top of them? What are the mountaintop experiences in our lives? Often a Christian will go away on a retreat and find the retreat center is located in the mountains. What is the significance of going up? Do we have an expectation that on the mountain we will meet the Lord? We know God is everywhere, yet somehow we feel closer to the divine the higher we climb.

In Exodus 33:18–23, Moses is called to the top of Mt. Sinai and he boldly asks to see the glory of God. Moses is gifted with a personal experience of the presence of the Almighty. He returns to the Israelites a changed person, his face radiant as a result of the encounter.

In 1 Kings 19:4–18, the prophet Elijah climbs the same mountain and also meets the Lord. He too is forever changed; he is emboldened by the experience. He returns to his ministry with renewed purpose and vigor.

Maybe that's what the mountaintop experience is about. We go up to meet the Lord and hope that when we return, when we come down the mountain, we will also be transformed by the experience. Peter, James, and John certainly were. Maybe it's time to plan that next retreat.

Oratio

This prayer helps us focus the power of the Transfiguration. *Radiant God, source of light, as you surround Jesus with your glory, so you come to us in penetrating brightness. You catch us off guard and expose our weakness. Fill us now with the courage to carry the good news into all the corners of the world and to bring back the joy of your presence off the mountain. Amen.*

Contemplatio

We all have to come down from the mountain. We return from "mountaintop experiences" to the normal order of our daily lives. The demands of everyday discipleship require us to come back to our workaday world. Can you take what you experienced on the mountain and allow it to transform the way you live your life as a believer this week? Peter, James, and John were sworn to secrecy until after the resurrection. We are not. We are free to announce to all that Jesus is alive and has transformed our lives. Ask the Lord to give you an opportunity this week to share with someone how the Lord has transformed you by a mountaintop experience of grace.

OTHER READINGS: GENESIS 22:1–2, 9a, 10–13, 15–18; ROMANS 8:31b–34

THIRD SUNDAY IN LENT

ZEAL FOR YOUR HOUSE

JOHN 2:13–25

[13] Since the Passover of the Jews was near, Jesus went up to Jerusalem.
[14] He found in the temple area those who sold oxen, sheep, and doves,
as well as the money-changers seated there. [15] He made a whip out of
cords and drove them all out of the temple area, with the sheep and

oxen, and spilled the coins of the money-changers and overturned
their tables, 16 and to those who sold doves he said, "Take these out of
here, and stop making my Father's house a marketplace." 17 His disciples recalled the words of scripture, "Zeal for your house will consume
me." 18 At this the Jews answered and said to him, "What sign can you
show us for doing this?" 19 Jesus answered and said to them, "Destroy
this temple and in three days I will raise it up." 20 The Jews said, "This
temple has been under construction for forty-six years, and you will
raise it up in three days?" 21 But he was speaking about the temple of
his body. 22 Therefore, when he was raised from the dead, his disciples
remembered that he had said this, and they came to believe the scripture and the word Jesus had spoken.

23 While he was in Jerusalem for the feast of Passover, many began to
believe in his name when they saw the signs he was doing. 24 But Jesus
would not trust himself to them because he knew them all, 25 and did not
need anyone to testify about human nature. He himself understood it well.

Lectio

In this week's Gospel Jesus travels to Jerusalem for the Passover feast. This annual pilgrimage was a time of great celebration. Jesus and his disciples are going up to Jerusalem to offer the prescribed sacrificial offering to the Lord and share together the best meal of the year.

Jesus arrives in Jerusalem and makes his way down the market street that stretches the length of the temple's western wall. This street is where local merchants sell the animals suitable for the Passover sacrifice. Money-changers stand ready to exchange currencies from any coinage stamped with graven images into the coinage of Israel that can then be used to make the offerings prescribed in the Law. Both services are certainly necessary. Jesus takes offense with these local merchants and money-changers because they are extorting their fellow Israelites. They raise the price of the sacrificial animals and offer a dishonest exchange rate. The whip of cords and the violent overturning of the tables are a warning to these merchants that they had better recalibrate their pricing and exchange rates before they see Jesus the following day.

The local population of religious leaders is shocked as much by this action as when Jesus refers to the temple as "my Father's house." They cannot believe what they have just heard. Jesus did not refer to the temple as "the Father's house" or as "our Father's house." Jesus personalizes the temple by referring to it as *his* Father's house. Jesus boldly asserts that he is the Son of God, the God who dwells in the temple! It is no wonder that the religious authorities challenge him to produce a sign to vindicate this bold claim. Jesus says that if they destroy this temple, in three days he will raise it back up. The Jerusalem temple had taken over forty-six years to reach its present-day glory. How could Jesus (or anyone) rebuild it in three days after it was destroyed? They do not understand that Jesus is speaking about his own body as the temple. His own body will be destroyed but his life will be restored after three days in the tomb. They don't understand this now, but some of them will. John reminds us that the disciples remembered this exchange and were inspired to believe the Scriptures and all the other words that Jesus had spoken to them since that first visit to Jerusalem.

Meditatio

When the disciples witness Jesus taking a whip of cords to the merchants and overturning the money-changers' tables they remember the words from Psalm 69: "Zeal for your house will consume me." King David's words emphasize that he had been insulted by others for his piety and spirited devotion to God.

Where is that kind of zeal in your life? What zeal consumes you these days? Has the expression of your zeal for God ever resulted in derision from others? It did for King David, so you are in good company.

And what does it mean to be *consumed* with this zeal? Is this a positive expression in the spiritual life? Meditate on the idea of holy zeal this week. Meditate on the idea of a holy zeal that will be expressed in actions of faith that draw us closer to the Lord. We don't need a whip of cords or the strength to overturn money-changers' tables. Our zeal can be expressed in our focused and dedicated attention to the Lord in the Word, in the church, and in our world.

Oratio

Let us pray with King David in Psalm 69:30–33 (NRSV) as we respond to the Lord in this week's Gospel: *"I will praise the name of God with a song; I will magnify him with thanksgiving. This will please the LORD more than an ox or a bull with horns and hoofs. Let the oppressed see it and be glad; you who seek God, let your hearts revive. For the LORD hears the needy, and does not despise his own that are in bonds."*

Contemplatio

In cleansing the temple, Jesus demonstrated to his disciples that he was concerned about correcting injustice. The "defect-free" animals needed for sacrificial offering were being sold at too high a price. Exchange rates were set in favor of the money-changers and the faithful pilgrim was losing out. Jesus acted to correct the situation so men and women could bring the best they could afford and offer those gifts to the Lord.

Where are the injustices in our world that God has given us the ability and influence to correct? Pray and ask the Lord to show you what you can do to restore justice in systems that can then work better to draw men and women to God. For Jesus that meant a reset on the market street leading to the temple entrance. What does it mean for you?

OTHER READINGS: EXODUS 20:1–17; 1 CORINTHIANS 1:22–25

FOURTH SUNDAY IN LENT

THE LIGHT CAME INTO THE WORLD

JOHN 3:14–21

14 "And just as Moses lifted up the serpent in the desert, so must the
Son of Man be lifted up, 15 so that everyone who believes in him may
have eternal life."

16 For God so loved the world that he gave his only Son, so that everyone who believes in him might not perish but might have eternal life.

[17] For God did not send his Son into the world to condemn the world,
but that the world might be saved through him. [18] Whoever believes in
him will not be condemned, but whoever does not believe has already
been condemned, because he has not believed in the name of the only
Son of God. [19] And this is the verdict, that the light came into the world,
but people preferred darkness to light, because their works were evil.
[20] For everyone who does wicked things hates the light and does not
come toward the light, so that his works might not be exposed. [21] But
whoever lives the truth comes to the light, so that his works may be
clearly seen as done in God.

Lectio

The setting of this Gospel is a late-night meeting between Jesus and Nicodemus, a recognized and honored leader of the Jewish temple authorities. Nicodemus has come to Jesus at night, not out of fear but rather to pursue a more meaningful and personal conversation with the wonder-worker from Galilee. The two meet beneath a canopy of olive branches, probably in the Garden of Gethsemane, and engage in an artful exchange in which Jesus tells Nicodemus that he must be "born again" if he is truly to understand who Jesus is and why he has come to Jerusalem.

Jesus honors Nicodemus as a teacher in Israel (like himself) and then draws his attention to a story from Numbers 21, where Moses crafts in bronze the image of a deadly serpent, mounts it on a pole, and lifts it high above the people, who are dying from the bites of venomous vipers. When a person looks at the bronze serpent, imaging the agent of death, they are healed. Jesus wants Nicodemus to know that the Son of Man (Jesus) will have to be lifted up (crucified) in similar manner so that all who look upon him crucified can be spared the finality of death.

Here the conversation between Jesus and Nicodemus comes to an end and a theological insight from our Gospel writer begins. The verses that follow are the words of the narrator, the apostle John, and not from the mouth of Jesus. John pauses here to summarize the purpose of Jesus's ministry. He reminds his community that God so loved the world that he sent his only Son to save it. God's vision is not one of condemnation but rather one of hope for all. The message of salvation and of being "born again" is for everyone.

John reminds us that Jesus is the light that has come into the world. That light became flesh and lived among us. Some people will love the darkness more than the light. For them there is little hope. But for those who respond to the gospel message and come toward the light, there is the promise of blessing and fellowship with God.

Meditatio

Why do we come to the light? As a child I visited the Colossal Cave complex in southern Arizona. At the lowest cave, the guide warned us that he was going to turn off the lights. We would be thrown into a darkness so complete it could be felt! I was extremely nervous when he flipped that switch and we were plunged into darkness deep below the surface of the earth. I will never forget my relief when the guide suddenly struck a match to illuminate the area around the light switch before flooding the cave again in artificial brilliance. I will never forget being drawn to that small but powerful light. For a brief moment it was my hope and comfort. I could not imagine turning away from that source of comfort.

What is it about light that is so compelling? To where does the darkness flee in the presence of light? We are all drawn to light. A city set on a hill cannot be hidden. Why do some reject the source of comfort to move deeper into darkness? This is a mystery and offers an opportunity for meditation this week.

Oratio

As a young freshman at Arizona State University I was invited to pray a prayer that changed the course of my life. It was called the "sinner's prayer" and is attributed to the evangelist Billy Graham. This prayer captured my heart's desire to be born again and to recommit myself to my walk with the Lord. This is the prayer that changed it all for me:

Dear Lord Jesus, I know that I am a sinner and I ask for your forgiveness. I believe you died for my sins and rose from the dead. I turn from my sins and invite you to come into my heart and life. I want to trust and follow you as my Lord and Savior. In your name, Amen.

Contemplatio

Our reading ends with a reference to "works" that have been "done in God." Here is where we put our faith into action. My friend Rabbi Michael is fond of reminding his Christian friends that "deeds trump creeds" in the outward expression of our faith. Doing the work of God and so witnessing God's presence in our lives is a powerful way to evangelize the nations. Our actions speak as loud as our words (or even louder). The world sees our faith in action and hopefully is drawn from their darkness toward the light of the Lord. Find a way this week to live out your faith in the good deeds that God provides for you to accomplish. Can you find a way to clothe the naked, feed the hungry, visit the sick, or bring comfort to someone in need? Pray that God will reveal to you many opportunities to let the light of your faith shine in the darkness of the world.

OTHER READINGS: 2 CHRONICLES 36:14–16, 19–23; EPHESIANS 2:4–10

FIFTH SUNDAY IN LENT

WHERE I AM, THERE ALSO WILL MY SERVANT BE

JOHN 12:20–33

20 Now there were some Greeks among those who had come up to
worship at the feast. 21 They came to Philip, who was from Bethsaida
in Galilee, and asked him, "Sir, we would like to see Jesus." 22 Philip
went and told Andrew; then Andrew and Philip went and told Jesus.
23 Jesus answered them, "The hour has come for the Son of Man to be
glorified. 24 Amen, amen, I say to you, unless a grain of wheat falls to
the ground and dies, it remains just a grain of wheat; but if it dies, it
produces much fruit. 25 Whoever loves his life loses it, and whoever
hates his life in this world will preserve it for eternal life. 26 Whoever
serves me must follow me, and where I am, there also will my servant
be. The Father will honor whoever serves me.

27 “I am troubled now. Yet what should I say? ‘Father, save me from this
hour’? But it was for this purpose that I came to this hour. 28 Father,
glorify your name.” Then a voice came from heaven, “I have glorified it and will glorify it again.” 29 The crowd there heard it and said it
was thunder; but others said, “An angel has spoken to him.” 30 Jesus
answered and said, “This voice did not come for my sake but for yours.
31 Now is the time of judgment on this world; now the ruler of this
world will be driven out. 32 And when I am lifted up from the earth,
I will draw everyone to myself.” 33 He said this indicating the kind of
death he would die.

Lectio

Huge crowds now surround Jesus. He has entered Jerusalem to the thunderous praise of multitudes who are equally enthralled by his latest and most powerful miracle to date, the calling forth of Lazarus from the grave. In this week's Gospel reading, Jesus is teaching on the temple mount when some Gentile converts to Judaism arrive in Jerusalem to celebrate the Passover feast. They find an apostle, Philip, and request that he take them to meet Jesus. They desire to know more about Jesus and want an opportunity to ask him questions specific to his ministry. Philip finds Andrew and together they bring these Greeks to Jesus. Jesus then proclaims publicly that his hour has now come, the hour for him to be glorified. What does he mean in referencing “this hour”?

We only hear one side of the conversation. John records the response of Jesus to the Greek converts. He says that yes, the hour has come for him to be glorified. He compares himself to a seed: a seed must die and be put into the ground before it can produce any fruit. No death and burial, no fruit—and for him, no glorification. It is that simple. Then Jesus tells the Greeks that if they want to serve him they have to be willing to follow him, even to the cross and then to the grave.

Jesus reveals that he is troubled and wonders aloud if he should ask the Father to deliver him from this hour. Jesus will be troubled as well in the Garden of Gethsemane. He is anticipating his suffering. He knows he has come to this hour to suffer and die an agonizing death on a cross before his body is placed in a tomb awaiting his resurrection. The hour that Jesus speaks of is the final week of his life, the completion of the journey that began three years earlier and ends at Golgotha.

God the Father honors the Son with a voice that thunders from heaven and Jesus announces that it is time for the ruler of the world to be driven out. Who is the ruler of this world? It is Satan, who controls men and women through the fear of death (see Hebrews 2:14–15). Jesus again reminds his followers that he will have to be "lifted up from the earth" (recall last week's reading from John 3), indicating to them the way he is going to die, by crucifixion. This is how he will draw everyone to himself.

Meditatio

Jesus speaks about love and hate when he reminds his disciples that "those who love their life lose it, and those who hate their life in this world will keep it for eternal life" (verse 25, NRSV).

The meaning of *love* and *hate* are different in this biblical context than you might have imagined. To "love" here means "to be attached to" and to "hate" in this context means "to become detached from." If we are going to follow Jesus we cannot be too attached to our life or we may lose it. To be authentic followers of Jesus we have to detach ourselves from selfish concerns (to hate our life in this world) as we anticipate the gift of eternal life on the other side of the grave. The only way to get from our point A to his point B is through death and resurrection. That's where Jesus is going and where he invites us to follow. Where he is, his servants—you and I—should also be. This is the way Jesus will honor the Father and the Father's plan of salvation. This is how we participate in that same plan and in the process draw others to Jesus. Ponder that this week.

Oratio

We will pray with St. Paul this week as we focus on the cross of our salvation:

"The message of the cross is foolishness to those who are perishing, but to us who are being saved it is the power of God." (1 Corinthians 1:18)

"But may I never boast except in the cross of our Lord Jesus Christ, through which the world has been crucified to me, and I to the world." (Galatians 6:14)

Lord, give me the courage to take up my cross and follow you this week as I continue on my journey through this Lenten season.

Contemplatio

How will we put our faith into action this week? In the Gospel reading we find Phillip and Andrew willing to bring the Greek converts to meet the Lord. Do people know us well enough to ask us how they can meet Jesus? Are we enough of a public witness to Jesus that when friends and family see us they know that we can take them to meet the Lord? Where would you take someone to meet Jesus? Could you invite someone to come to church with you this week? To your Bible study? To your fellowship group? To a family event that will evidence your faith in Jesus by the way you celebrate together? These are all ways that we can become Phillips and Andrews in the lives of those we know and love. Give it a try this week.

OTHER READINGS: JEREMIAH 31:31–34; HEBREWS 5:7–9

PALM SUNDAY

HOSANNA! SAVE US, LORD!

MARK 11:1–10

1 When they drew near to Jerusalem, to Bethphage and Bethany at the
Mount of Olives, he sent two of his disciples 2 and said to them, "Go
into the village opposite you, and immediately on entering it, you will
find a colt tethered on which no one has ever sat. Untie it and bring
it here. 3 If anyone should say to you, 'Why are you doing this?' reply,
'The Master has need of it and will send it back here at once.'" 4 So they
went off and found a colt tethered at a gate outside on the street, and
they untied it. 5 Some of the bystanders said to them, "What are you
doing, untying the colt?" 6 They answered them just as Jesus had told
them to, and they permitted them to do it. 7 So they brought the colt
to Jesus and put their cloaks over it. And he sat on it. 8 Many people
spread their cloaks on the road, and others spread leafy branches that

they had cut from the fields. 9 Those preceding him as well as those following kept crying out:

"Hosanna! Blessed is he who comes in the name of the Lord!
10 Blessed is the kingdom of our father David that is to come!
Hosanna in the highest!"

Lectio

Palm Sunday is here and the Mass will begin with the reading of this Gospel as the faithful gather outside the church. We will each hold a palm frond as we anticipate processing into the church with joy. The original celebration took place on the Mount of Olives as Jesus prepared to enter Jerusalem and then visit the temple. This Palm Sunday event is recorded in all four Gospels. The procession down the Mount of Olives and into Jerusalem was the culmination anticipated by the huge crowd that thronged to Jesus and led him in their midst into the holy city.

Jesus is clearly in charge of this triumphant procession. He knows that many among the most zealous in the crowd want to anoint him as the new king of Israel. He has to find a way to dampen their militaristic zeal. They have cut palm branches for themselves on their way through Jericho (the City of Palms) in anticipation of waving them victoriously as they follow their Messiah, Jesus, to his rightful place on the throne as the King of Israel! Since the time of the Maccabees (see 1 Maccabees 13:51) the palm branch has been associated with the military victory over the Greek overlords who had defiled the temple. In the Maccabees narrative the temple is taken back from the Greeks. Palm branches were used in a liturgical gesture of sweeping, showing that the Greeks had been deposed—swept away—and the temple and its sacrifices were now restored. Jesus knew in advance of his arrival in Bethany that the crowds were ready to wave those branches again in open defiance of the Roman soldiers who would line the route to the temple as keepers of the peace.

This background explains the arrangements made in advance to have a she-donkey available to convey Jesus humbly into the city. He knows that riding this beast of burden will fulfill the prophecy of Zechariah 9:9 and confound the Roman guard, who would see the scene as only comical.

The crowds will have none of this. They try to give Jesus the "red carpet" treatment by throwing their cloaks over the back of the donkey and even on the road that Jesus will travel upon. Still, the Roman soldiers would perceive no threat here.

The chants of the crowd, most certainly in Aramaic, would also have been unintelligible to the Romans. Hosanna translates to "Save us, we pray!" Jesus is the one who comes in the name of our Lord, not the so-called Lord of the Earth, Caesar! Hosanna—save us, O most high one in heaven—is a cry for God to intervene quickly in the affairs of the people. The Roman authorities do not understand the politically charged rhetoric directed toward them as the crowds pass by. It seems to them just another procession of joyful Jews coming to worship their God in the temple. Crisis avoided. Jesus saves the day and Holy Week begins.

Meditatio

In practicing Lectio Divina, we are expected to read and re-read the Gospel and allow certain words to rise up and speak to us each week. This week the word that caught my attention is Hosanna! It is a one-word prayer. The writer of Psalm 118, a victory psalm, prays for God to "save us [hosanna]" and "give us success!" (118:25). The psalmist has called to the Lord in distress but with the confident assurance that God will save and set the psalmist on a level place (118:5). The psalm is a song of victory over enemies, celebrating the restoration of the "stone that the builders rejected" that "has become the chief cornerstone" (118:22 NRSV).

The cry of Hosanna captures this energy, then and now. It is a prayer of confident assurance in our God who sees, our God who hears, our God who saves. Hosanna! Save us, Lord! This is a single-word prayer we can offer in a time of need—and a one-word shout of praise we can offer to the Lord in thanksgiving.

Oratio

This week Psalm 24 captures the joy of anticipation as pilgrims march toward the temple in the time of Jesus. It was a time of celebration and joy! This Psalm could have been sung on Palm Sunday 2000 years ago:

"Lift up your heads, O gates! and be lifted up, O ancient doors! that the King of glory may come in. Who is the King of glory? The Lord, strong and mighty, the Lord, mighty in battle." (Psalm 24:7–8 NRSV).

Contemplatio

Jesus sent two disciples into Bethany to collect the donkey that he was going to ride into Jerusalem. These two put his faith in them into action. Jesus had warned them that if anyone asked them what they were doing they were to respond that, "The Master has need of it and will send it back here at once." They find the animal and do just as Jesus has directed.

What do we have that the Lord might need? Are we willing to give to him what he asks of us? What gift or talent has God blessed you with that can be used to bring the light of the gospel into your world? Do you sing? Are you gifted as an administrator? Can you raise funds? How about helping to clean up after church events? If there is a need, can the Lord count on you to fill in with your gifts this week? Be open to these sort opportunities and they will come.

OTHER READINGS: ISAIAH 50:4–7; PHILIPPIANS 2:8–9; MARK 14:1—15:47

THE RESURRECTION OF THE LORD

THE FIRST DAY OF THE WEEK

JOHN 20:1–9

1 On the first day of the week, Mary of Magdala came to the tomb early
in the morning, while it was still dark, and saw the stone removed
from the tomb. 2 So she ran and went to Simon Peter and to the other
disciple whom Jesus loved, and told them, "They have taken the Lord
from the tomb, and we don't know where they put him." 3 So Peter
and the other disciple went out and came to the tomb. 4 They both ran,
but the other disciple ran faster than Peter and arrived at the tomb
first; 5 he bent down and saw the burial cloths there, but did not go in.
6 When Simon Peter arrived after him, he went into the tomb and saw

the burial cloths there, [7] and the cloth that had covered his head, not
with the burial cloths but rolled up in a separate place. [8] Then the other
disciple also went in, the one who had arrived at the tomb first, and he
saw and believed. [9] For they did not yet understand the scripture that
he had to rise from the dead.

Lectio

The Gospel opens on Sunday, the first day of the Jewish week. Jewish time is based on a lunar calculation. The "day" begins and ends at sundown. This is the day of the Resurrection! The Passover celebration is complete. Mary of Magdala and some other women have brought aromatic burial spices to the tomb to prepare the body of Jesus for transport, most likely back to Nazareth. They arrive early in the morning to find that the stone sealing the tomb has been rolled away, the Roman guard has gone missing, and the tomb is empty. Shocked, Mary suspects theft and runs to Peter and the other disciples, in hiding nearby in the upper room where the Passover meal had been celebrated only a few nights earlier.

Mary finds them and announces her news to Peter and "the other disciple whom Jesus loved"—a character most identify as the author of this Gospel, John. Both run to the tomb. John, the youngest apostle, is swifter than Peter and arrives at the entrance of the tomb first. He peers inside, but waits until Peter arrives. John watches as Peter enters and carefully examines the interior or the tomb. Peter must have beckoned John to enter. When he does, John sees enough to know that Jesus has somehow cheated death and conquered the grave. John "saw and believed"!

There was still some doubt to sort out—there always is and always will be. John shares with his readers that they still did not understand that Scripture taught that the Messiah had to suffer and die before he returned from the dead. But Peter and John leave the scene as believers. The tomb is empty. He is risen! He is risen indeed!

Meditatio

In this account of the empty tomb, Peter and John run to arrive at the scene. They "saw" the empty tomb and the grave clothes. Peter noticed that the wrappings from the head of Jesus were not lying with the other burial material. What did they conclude from this evidence that they saw?

In our English translation, we note that both Peter and John "saw" aspects of the scene and conclude from what they saw that Jesus had risen from the grave. It is interesting that in the original Greek the writer uses three separate words to describe how they saw and understood the evidence of the empty tomb. John arrives at the entrance of the tomb and "saw" that it was empty. Our author uses the word *blepo* to describe that experience. To *blepo* means to simply see what is before you. Then Peter arrives and goes into the tomb, and we learn that he "saw" more evidence than John. Here the Greek word for seeing is *thereo,* which means that he is beginning to attach additional meaning (forming a theory) beyond what he sees on the surface. Then John enters the tomb and "saw" all that Peter saw—but now the Greek word used for sight is *eido.* This indicates that John came to an intelligent conclusion based on the evidence. Now we know why John writes that he "saw and believed."

Our journey of faith is similar. We have to come into contact with a set of facts, give them careful consideration, and wait for the Spirit to confirm those facts to us so that we can believe. This takes time, perhaps even a period of forty days in anticipation of Holy Week and Easter. Faith is a process of growth. This is confirmed in this resurrection account.

Oratio

St. Paul relates an early Christian prayer when he writes to the church in Ephesus. This prayer is a call for the believer to wake up and allow the light of Jesus to shine so that you can live a full life of faith. It will be our prayer this week: "Sleeper, awake! Rise from the dead, and Christ will shine on you" (Ephesians 5:14 NRSV). Christ is risen! He is risen indeed!

Contemplatio

How can we put our faith into action this week? One way would be to follow the example of Mary of Magdala, Peter, and John in their willingness to run to the tomb and peer inside. Where are the places that announce the resurrection (the empty tomb) in our life? To where could we run? We could decide to run to the church and make plans to attend all the liturgies of the Triduum during Holy Week. Clear your schedule in advance so that you can be present for liturgies on Holy Thursday, Good Friday, and Holy Saturday. Make those liturgies your experience of "running to the tomb," and pray that Jesus will reveal himself to you in a brand new way so that you, like the beloved disciple in the Gospel, can also "see and believe" before you return to your home.

OTHER READINGS: ACTS 10:34a, 37–43; COLOSSIANS 3:1–4

SECOND SUNDAY OF EASTER

HEARING AND BELIEVING

JOHN 20:19–31

19 On the evening of that first day of the week, when the doors were
locked, where the disciples were, for fear of the Jews, Jesus came and
stood in their midst and said to them, "Peace be with you." 20 When
he had said this, he showed them his hands and his side. The disciples
rejoiced when they saw the Lord. 21 [Jesus] said to them again, "Peace
be with you. As the Father has sent me, so I send you." 22 And when
he had said this, he breathed on them and said to them, "Receive the
holy Spirit. 23 Whose sins you forgive are forgiven them, and whose
sins you retain are retained."

24 Thomas, called Didymus, one of the Twelve, was not with them when
Jesus came. 25 So the other disciples said to him, "We have seen the
Lord." But he said to them, "Unless I see the mark of the nails in his
hands and put my finger into the nailmarks and put my hand into his
side, I will not believe." 26 Now a week later his disciples were again
inside and Thomas was with them. Jesus came, although the doors
were locked, and stood in their midst and said, "Peace be with you."
27 Then he said to Thomas, "Put your finger here and see my hands, and
bring your hand and put it into my side, and do not be unbelieving, but
believe." 28 Thomas answered and said to him, "My Lord and my God!"

[29] Jesus said to him, "Have you come to believe because you have seen me? Blessed are those who have not seen and have believed."

[30] Now Jesus did many other signs in the presence of [his] disciples that are not written in this book. [31] But these are written that you may [come to] believe that Jesus is the Messiah, the Son of God, and that through this belief you may have life in his name.

Lectio

This is the post-resurrection narrative that we typically associate with "Doubting Thomas." We are reminded in this passage that the apostle Thomas is called "Didymus," which loosely translates to "twin." In Christian tradition it has been suggested that he bore a striking resemblance to Jesus. This may explain why Judas makes arrangements with the guard sent to arrest Jesus that he will identify the Lord with a kiss in Gethsemane. They needed to apprehend the right man in the darkness of the olive grove.

The first scene is set on the day of Jesus's resurrection. Thomas is not present with the other disciples, who are huddling behind locked doors in the upper room in (understandable) fear of reprisal from the Jewish authorities who had tried Jesus and handed him over to Pontius Pilate to be crucified. Jesus appears and reveals himself as the risen Lord. He invites the disciples to come forward and to probe the wounds in his hands and side. We have to assume that many take him up on the offer and realize that Jesus is the same person they witnessed on the cross and saw placed in the tomb only three days earlier. That's what they keep telling Thomas over the next week.

Where Thomas was on that particular Sunday night remains a mystery, but a week later we find him back with the disciples in the same place, and Jesus again appears. He speaks directly to Thomas and offers Thomas the same opportunity to examine his wounds as he had the previous Sunday. Thomas, no doubter here, simply exclaims, "My Lord and my God." His is a bold statement of heartfelt faith, and an example for us.

A careful reading of the text this week reveals Thomas not as a doubter but rather the first of many who will see and believe. Jesus congratulates Thomas for believing without having to probe the wounds of the

crucifixion. Then he goes on: Blessed, Jesus says, will be all those after Thomas who will come to faith without even having to see. They will hear and believe.

Meditatio

On what Sunday would you have preferred to encounter the risen Jesus? On that first day of the week you would be offered an opportunity to attest to the physical presence of Jesus as you examine his body and probe the depth of the wounds presented to you in his hands and side. You see, you examine closely, and you come to faith.

One week later you could find yourself in the same situation. This time you would be present with Thomas and any others among the core group of disciples who had not yet seen Jesus. Jesus greets you and offers you the opportunity to touch and probe in just the same way that the others had before. On this Sunday evening you see and believe.

In both encounters with the risen Jesus men and women come to faith. Thomas becomes an example for us of those who believe without the need of physical proof. He is the bridge from Jesus to you and me. Unlike Thomas we believe based not on what we have seen but rather on what we have heard, and we are called blessed by the Lord.

Oratio

I am reminded of a Gospel account of a healing afforded a father for his son. The father begs Jesus for compassion and help in setting his son free from an evil spirit. Jesus responds by saying that "everything is possible to one who has faith," to which the man then exclaims, "I do believe, help my unbelief!" (Mark 9:23–24).

As we take the Gospel to prayer this week let's recall that sometimes authentic belief comes in stages and by degrees. Whatever level of faith we know today can grow into a deeper reality over time. "I do believe, help my unbelief!" for you are "My Lord and my God!"

Contemplatio

We end each Lectio experience with the challenge to put our faith into action. Jesus honors Thomas for coming to faith as the result of what he has seen. He then says that all who come after Thomas, those who will believe without the benefit of seeing the risen Lord, are to be called blessed as well. That's us!

Be aware this week that you are a living witness of the Gospel. As a Christian your life becomes a witness to those who have not seen Jesus but can meet him when they meet you. We know that Jesus is our Lord and our God. He is our teacher and the divine Son of the Father. When others see us joyfully living our faith they will be drawn to him. In this way seeing is believing—when seeing includes others watching and listening to the good news that our lives proclaim.

OTHER READINGS: ACTS 4:32–35; 1 JOHN 5:1–6

THIRD SUNDAY OF EASTER

PEACE BE WITH YOU

LUKE 24:35–48

35 Then the two recounted what had taken place on the way and how he
was made known to them in the breaking of the bread.

36 While they were still speaking about this, he stood in their midst
and said to them, "Peace be with you." 37 But they were startled and
terrified and thought that they were seeing a ghost. 38 Then he said to
them, "Why are you troubled? And why do questions arise in your
hearts? 39 Look at my hands and my feet, that it is I myself. Touch me
and see, because a ghost does not have flesh and bones as you can see
I have." 40 And as he said this, he showed them his hands and his feet.
41 While they were still incredulous for joy and were amazed, he asked
them, "Have you anything here to eat?" 42 They gave him a piece of
baked fish; 43 he took it and ate it in front of them.

44 He said to them, "These are my words that I spoke to you while I was
still with you, that everything written about me in the law of Moses
and in the prophets and psalms must be fulfilled." 45 Then he opened

their minds to understand the scriptures. 46 And he said to them, "Thus
it is written that the Messiah would suffer and rise from the dead on
the third day 47 and that repentance, for the forgiveness of sins, would
be preached in his name to all the nations, beginning from Jerusalem.
48 You are witnesses of these things."

Lectio

The Gospel opens as the two disciples who met Jesus on the road to Emmaus are sharing the story of their post-resurrection encounter with the Twelve in the upper room. They recognized him "in the breaking of the bread." They have returned to Jerusalem that very night to find the disciples hiding behind closed doors in fear of the Jewish authorities who had condemned Jesus to death. They share their experience with the risen Lord. In the time they spent with Jesus, he had opened the Scriptures to them and shown them that, as the true Messiah, he was destined to suffer and die before his promised return from the grave. The two from the Emmaus road were "evangelizing" the community of believers that night.

As they are speaking, Jesus himself appears and greets them all with a single word: *Shalom* (translated to *eirene* in Greek). It means, "May the peace of God come upon you all." The disciples are terrified. They are sure they are looking at a ghost. Jesus invites them to examine his body, to probe the wounds the nails left in his hands, to examine where the spear pierced his side. We have to assume that the disciples did exactly that. They become convinced that this is the risen Jesus who stands before them in the "flesh." Jesus confirms his true presence when he asks for food and drink. A ghost cannot eat. This is the final proof the disciples need. Jesus the Messiah has conquered death and the grave!

Jesus opens the Word to them. What a Bible class that must have been. He uses texts from the Old Testament to recall all that has been written about him in the Law (the first five books of the Old Testament), the Prophets (all of those who spoke in the name of the Lord in the Old Testament), and the Psalms (a term that covers the wisdom literature of the Hebrew Bible). Jesus "opened their minds" so that they could understand how all these texts referred to him.

The mission is now clear. This message of salvation is to be proclaimed to all the nations. The Gentiles are going to hear the plan of God to include them in the mercy of salvation. The message of good news will eventually reach the ends of the earth. Then the disciples are instructed to stay in the city of Jerusalem until the promised "power from on high" descends upon them. The passage anticipates the celebration of Pentecost that follows fifty days after the Passover concludes. The stage is set. The final piece of the puzzle is in place. Forty days of training lie ahead. Watch, world, for nothing will ever be the same again. Here we come!

Meditatio

When we read the Gospel through the lens of the Lectio Divina method we trust that the Holy Spirit will draw our attention to a word or a phrase that will be the source of our meditation each week. For this Gospel passage the word for me is *shalom,* which loosely translates into English as, "Peace be with you." Shalom means so much more than a simple wish for peace, a hope for the absence of conflict or strife. The root of the word in Hebrew is *shalam,* which means "to be safe in mind, in body, and in your world." Shalom envisages a type of wholeness that encourages you to give back, to generously repay something to someone in some way. It is an "action" word that conveys God's intent for our lives.

You use the word *shalom* in Israel today when you greet or say goodbye to someone. It is a wish of fullness and well-being. On the lips of Jesus, "shalom" becomes a prayer that hope, health, and prosperity will come upon those assembled in the upper room. That's the powerful meaning behind a simple greeting. Jesus is wishing his disciples wholeness and well-being in this moment of fright and doubt. We are called to wish that same blessing to all we meet and serve this week.

Oratio

As I lead a tour through the land of Israel this month, I am drawn to two verses about the shalom of God that I teach on the opening morning of the trip on the Mount of Beatitudes and when we remember Jesus and his entry into Jerusalem from the heights of the Mount of Olives. Our prayer response this week will be a reflection on these two texts:

Matthew 5:9: *"Blessed are the peacemakers, for they will be called children of God."* Psalm 122:6–7: *"For the peace of Jerusalem pray: 'May those who love you prosper! May peace be within your ramparts, prosperity within your towers.'"*

Contemplatio

In the Gospel Jesus offers the disciples physical evidence that he is really present among them after the resurrection by showing them his hands and his feet and inviting them to probe the wounds the crucifixion left on his body. Jesus has asked us to be his hands and feet. When we put our faith into action this week we will reveal the resurrected Jesus to people who might otherwise doubt.

The lives we live as believers should be a witness to who we are as followers of Jesus. We have to find ways to go where he would go and to do what he would do. We become witnesses when we enter the world of others and show them that Jesus is real, real in you and me, as we show our faith in the way we live. We witness in the way we treat them, the way we treat each other. We have already received the promised power from on high—the Holy Spirit. That is the secret to our success in being a living witness of Jesus this week. Lean into the Holy Spirit and pray for opportunities that will allow you to show those in doubt that Jesus is alive and that he lives in you.

OTHER READINGS: ACTS 3:13–15, 17–19; 1 JOHN 2:1–5a

FOURTH SUNDAY OF EASTER

THE GOOD SHEPHERD

JOHN 10:11–18

[11] "I am the good shepherd. A good shepherd lays down his life for the
sheep. [12] A hired man, who is not a shepherd and whose sheep are
not his own, sees a wolf coming and leaves the sheep and runs away,
and the wolf catches and scatters them. [13] This is because he works

for pay and has no concern for the sheep. [14] I am the good shepherd,
and I know mine and mine know me, [15] just as the Father knows me
and I know the Father; and I will lay down my life for the sheep. [16] I
have other sheep that do not belong to this fold. These also I must lead,
and they will hear my voice, and there will be one flock, one shepherd.
[17] This is why the Father loves me, because I lay down my life in order
to take it up again. [18] No one takes it from me, but I lay it down on my
own. I have power to lay it down, and power to take it up again. This
command I have received from my Father."

Lectio

Jesus was raised in the ridgetop village of Nazareth. There he learned the ways of construction from his adoptive father Joseph and also became familiar with another way people made a living. The hill country around Nazareth is uniquely suited for the pasturing of flocks, both sheep and goats, and Jesus knew and understood the ways of the shepherd. Consider the challenge Jesus has before him in today's passage. He is teaching his disciples about himself by drawing on shepherding practices from the hill country. But these metaphors would be somewhat foreign to many of them who worked the Sea of Galilee as commercial fishermen.

Jesus proclaims to his disciples that he is a good shepherd who lays down his life for his sheep. He compares this good shepherd to the hired man who runs at the first sight of danger and leaves the flock vulnerable to local predators. How does a shepherd lay down his life for the sheep? He does so, paradoxically, when he leaves the rest of the flock and goes out in search of a lost animal. This is done at great risk to the shepherd because that sheep he is looking for has likely become "cast down" due to the weight of the wool it is carrying. That sheep is unable to turn over and stand up. It cries out in despair. This mournful bleating is the dinner bell for any nearby wolf. The good shepherd is willing to risk his own life to seek out and save a single lost sheep. The shepherd is looking for the same animal that the predators are also seeking to find. Who will arrive on the scene first? In a display of supreme bravery the good shepherd will imperil himself to seek out, find, and return the lost animal to the flock.

Ancient and modern shepherds in the Middle East train the animals in their flocks to respond to specific whistles and sounds. I have witnessed ten sheep called out from a group of hundreds. These animals knew their own shepherd's voice and responded to his call. There is a depth of intimacy between the sheep and the shepherd. The animals will only respond to their shepherd. Jesus knows that the sheep of his flock know his voice and will follow him where he will lead.

Meditatio

Jesus teaches the disciples that the Father loves him because he lays down his life for the sheep. Our good shepherd will lay down his life when he goes out in search of the lost sheep. Because he is willing to risk his life for the flock the Father will honor him.

Then there are the sheep that do not belong to his fold. Jesus says he must lead them as well. They must learn to listen to the call of a new shepherd and join the one flock. Who are the sheep that don't yet belong to our flock? How can we be the voice of Jesus that they hear as an invitation to join the one flock of the one shepherd?

The Father knows Jesus and he knows the Father. That intimate relationship gives him the confidence he needs to lay down his life. This is the same relationship that will give us the confidence to follow the example of our good shepherd.

Oratio

King David was a good shepherd too. In Psalm 23 he reflects on the responsibility that a good shepherd has for his flock. At the end of our prayer this week you will see the phrase "he restores my soul." This is how, as the shepherd finds and rescues a sheep that has become "cast down," he also saves the life of the lost sheep.

"The Lord is my shepherd; there is nothing I lack. In green pastures he makes me lie down; to still waters he leads me; he restores my soul."

Contemplatio

Am I a good shepherd or a hired man? What is my response to threats to the flock in my pastoral care? I am a husband, a father, a grandfather. I want to be a good shepherd to all of these “flocks” in my life. How about you? Where has God put you in a position of pastoral influence? Do you love the flock in your care? When we find ourselves in positions of leadership and influence, do we take on the character of the good shepherd or flee from challenges we should be willing to face?

There is safety in numbers. It is good to be the member of a large flock. Still, we have to be aware of those who need our help to come back to the fold and the care of the good shepherd. Ask the Lord to show you whom you should reach out to this week. Invite them back into the blessing of the flock that is our church community today. Take the challenge and reach out to the “other sheep” this week.

OTHER READINGS: ACTS 4:8–12; 1 JOHN 3:1–2;

FIFTH SUNDAY OF EASTER

THAT YOU BEAR MUCH FRUIT

JOHN 15:1–8

1 “I am the true vine, and my Father is the vine grower. 2 He takes away
every branch in me that does not bear fruit, and every one that does
he prunes so that it bears more fruit. 3 You are already pruned because
of the word that I spoke to you. 4 Remain in me, as I remain in you.
Just as a branch cannot bear fruit on its own unless it remains on the
vine, so neither can you unless you remain in me. 5 I am the vine, you
are the branches. Whoever remains in me and I in him will bear much
fruit, because without me you can do nothing. 6 Anyone who does not
remain in me will be thrown out like a branch and wither; people will
gather them and throw them into a fire and they will be burned. 7 If
you remain in me and my words remain in you, ask for whatever you
want and it will be done for you. 8 By this is my Father glorified, that
you bear much fruit and become my disciples.”

The vine and branches is an ancient motif for the Jewish people, going back to the prophet Isaiah (Isaiah 5:1–5) and the vision of God planting a vineyard on a hill that God will tend and care for and will eventually call Israel. Although that vineyard only yields wild grapes the Father continues to hold the vineyard of Israel close in care and concern.

The Gospel for this week opens as Jesus moves with his disciples across the temple mount. He stops the group of disciples in front of the doorway that leads to the inner temple area. Carved into the façade of this portal is a fruitful vine and healthy branches in relief. From this vantage point Jesus declares that he is the true vine and that his Father is the vine grower. The chief goal of the vinedresser is to produce an abundant harvest of fruit, but this goal requires time to achieve—and involves yearly pruning of the vine. This kind of pruning is an exacting practice. It appears to the uninitiated that the vinedresser has cut away too much of the vine, but this expert work will produce even more fruit the following year.

The counsel of Jesus to the disciples is to remain in the vine because no branch can produce fruit by itself. Jesus is on his way to Gethsemane where nearly all of these disciples will desert him in an effort to save their own lives. Jesus reminds them here to remember the lesson of vine and branches. Pruning has to be done to ensure greater growth in the future.

Jesus concludes his reflection with the promise that if the disciples remain in him, and his teaching guides their lives, then they can ask for whatever they want and it will be granted to them by the Father. The branch that is attached to the vine knows how to produce fruit. The disciple connected to Jesus will know that same blessing.

Jesus is revealing the Father to the disciples as a Middle Eastern patron. In the Middle East those who have power (patrons) are expected to use it to serve others in a generous manner. It brings honor to the patron when clients (here the disciples) come with requests that only the patron can fulfill. There is no expectation of payment for the blessings they receive. The client is expected to honor the patron with praise and thanksgiving. It is the patron's good pleasure to bless the clients in this way.

Meditatio

"By this is my Father glorified, that you bear much fruit and become my disciples." How can we glorify God? It seems presumptuous on our part as disciples to try and give God glory. We are creatures and God is the creator. It should be God who gives the glory. We need to allow Middle Eastern culture to inform our understanding of this passage. The word that we see translated as "glorified" can also be translated as "honored," which may be easier to comprehend in the context of Jesus's teaching.

Honor is the primary Middle Eastern value. Honor drives the culture. You are born into a certain "honor status" at birth and are expected to maintain that level for the whole of your life. Honor is a "public claim to value and worth" that is acknowledged by members of the family, village, community, and nation.

When we are securely connected to the vine as a healthy, fruit-producing branch we bring honor to the Father. It will please the Father to see us bearing good fruit. This is how we can glorify the Father. We can't do this on our own. Our openness to the strength the vine provides the branches is evidence that we are living in and through the might of the Father who is our Patron. God is glorified, God is honored, when we bear the good fruit that is the result of our staying connected to the true vine. When we reveal the good fruit in our lives we bring honor to the Father, who delights to provide all we need to live as children of the light in a world much too comfortable in darkness.

Oratio

I was drawn to this prayer from *Our Daily Bread.* "Thank you, Lord, for nurturing us with your truth, dwelling within us, and empowering us to enjoy a life of fruitfulness. Cultivate grace and courage in our hearts. Prune us with gentle hands so that we will bloom, as we obey your Word and praise you with reckless abandon. Amen."

Contemplatio

Jesus teaches the disciples that when they bear much fruit they bring honor to the Father. The same holds true for you and me. What kind of fruit should we be looking to produce? In the letter to the Galatians St. Paul provides insight when he writes that the fruit of the Spirit is love, joy, peace, patience, kindness, generosity, faithfulness, gentleness, and self-control (Galatians 5:22–23). This a good working list as we consider how to put the Gospel into practice this week. The first fruit that St. Paul mentions is love. In the Bible *love* includes the meaning of "connection." This ties in nicely with the vine and branches imagery. Jesus wants us to remain in him, as he remains in us. It can take significant attention and effort to stay connected to one another. Use this week to try and build a stronger bond between yourself and Jesus. Make the extra effort to "remain in him" through your personal and public expression of faith. This is one more way we can bear fruit in our lives and honor the Father.

OTHER READINGS: ACTS 9:26–31; 1 JOHN 3:18–24

SIXTH SUNDAY OF EASTER

REMAIN IN MY LOVE

JOHN 15:9–17

> 9 "As the Father loves me, so I also love you. Remain in my love. 10 If you
> keep my commandments, you will remain in my love, just as I have
> kept my Father's commandments and remain in his love.
>
> 11 "I have told you this so that my joy may be in you and your joy may
> be complete. 12 This is my commandment: love one another as I love
> you. 13 No one has greater love than this, to lay down one's life for one's
> friends. 14 You are my friends if you do what I command you. 15 I no
> longer call you slaves, because a slave does not know what his master
> is doing. I have called you friends, because I have told you everything I
> have heard from my Father. 16 It was not you who chose me, but I who
> chose you and appointed you to go and bear fruit that will remain, so
> that whatever you ask the Father in my name he may give you. 17 This
> I command you: love one another."

In this reading Jesus uses the word "love" nine times in nine verses! You might say that love is important to Jesus, as is our ability to understand the meaning of the term as it functions in the Middle Eastern world of the Bible. If we are to be authentic disciples and servants of the Lord, we have to understand what Jesus means when he calls us to love one another.

Our Middle Eastern ancestors in the faith used the word love differently than we do in the West. In the Bible, love has a deeper meaning than the emotional feelings we normally attach to the word. Jesus uses "love" to convey a concept of attachment and bonding to a particular group of people, most notably the members of a family. To love one another is to stay connected with the others in the group, and to do whatever it takes to maintain the bond that expresses that unity.

In John 13:35 Jesus teaches his disciples that it is the love they express toward one another that will witness to the world that they belong to him, that he is their teacher. This is his new commandment, that the disciples love one another. Jesus expresses the depth of his love by his willingness to lay down his life for the disciples, whom he now refers to as his friends.

Jesus calling the disciples his friends is no small matter. In the Old Testament even some of the greatest characters in salvation history are not called friends by God. Moses (Deuteronomy 34:5), Joshua (Joshua 24:29), and even David (Psalm 89:21) are all known as servants of God but are not called God's friends. The title of "friend of God" is reserved to Abraham (Isaiah 41:8). But now the term is used by Jesus to refer to the disciples.

The title "friend" conveys the attachment that Jesus feels for the disciples and the connection that they should have with one another. The command is simple. Love one another. But how? We learn that we are called to follow the example of Jesus, who is willing to lay down his life for his friends. St. Paul reminds us in Romans 13:10 that "Love does no evil to the neighbor; hence love is the fulfillment of the law." When we love one another, when we are willing to lay down our lives for each other, that is when the law is fulfilled. That is when the joy the Lord promises the disciples will be realized in our lives.

Meditatio

Love is a verb. It is an action word in the Bible. It demands a response to be fully realized. In the Middle Eastern world, males have generally been more interested in "being" rather than "doing." Middle Eastern men have normally opted to respond spontaneously to the present moment, trusting that their response is appropriate. Jesus expected men to hear a joyous song and dance, or to hear a dirge and mourn (Matthew 11:16–17). But sometimes men would become complacent in their "being" and neglect the "doing" that daily life requires. This is one place that the challenge of love enters the spiritual equation. Love is active: it is something that we must choose to do. It takes effort to love, to stay connected to others.

Where Middle Eastern men would rather "be" than "do" and so may need encouragement to love in an active way, Middle Eastern women have operated on a different wavelength. Consider Martha, the close friend of Jesus who was always ready to "do" in service to others. Jesus encouraged her to slow down and to "be" like her sister Mary, who was invited to sit at the feet of Jesus and learn from him as a disciple (Luke 10:38–42).

Jesus commands us to love one another. This is a call to action. We have to work to stay connected to each other. This is our witness to the world outside the church. When the world sees how we love one another as brothers and sisters in Christ they will be drawn to join the family of faith.

Oratio

Joy is a hallmark of the Christian. The joy we experience in knowing the Lord is something that we can easily share with others around us. This is one way that the world will know that we have been born again. Pray for this holy joy this week: *Lord I thank you for the gift of your love in my life. I ask that I can know the joy that you promised me as your child and that I can know this joy in its fullest expression. Make that joy in me complete.*

Contemplatio

The call to love in the Gospel is a call to action. The paradox in our lives is that we are often too engaged and active to take moments aside to sit quietly and just "be" in the presence of the Lord.

That will be our challenge this week. We need to find a time and a place where we can slow down and do nothing other than rest in the Lord. This is a time we can look forward to each day—time spent with the Lord in the Word or in quiet and personal prayer, time where we can recharge our spiritual batteries so we can be a more effective witness to the transformation that has called us from darkness into the light of faith.

Jesus says that he now calls us his friends. Friends take time to be present to one another. Friends take time to sit and listen to the other. Friends look forward to spending this time together. Lean into this aspect of our friendship with God this week. Ask God to help us express our being in the love of God by acting as God's friends in the world.

OTHER READINGS: ACTS 10:25–26, 34–35, 44–48; 1 JOHN 4:7–10

ASCENSION OF THE LORD

GO INTO THE WHOLE WORLD AND PROCLAIM

MARK 16:15–20

15 He said to them, "Go into the whole world and proclaim the gospel to
every creature. 16 Whoever believes and is baptized will be saved; whoever does not believe will be condemned. 17 These signs will accompany
those who believe: in my name they will drive out demons, they will
speak new languages. 18 They will pick up serpents [with their hands],
and if they drink any deadly thing, it will not harm them. They will lay
hands on the sick, and they will recover."

19 So then the Lord Jesus, after he spoke to them, was taken up into
heaven and took his seat at the right hand of God. 20 But they went
forth and preached everywhere, while the Lord worked with them and
confirmed the word through accompanying signs.

This week we will celebrate the Feast of the Ascension. We remember how Jesus spent the first forty days after his resurrection training the apostles and the other disciples. Then he ascended into heaven from the top of the Mount of Olives. The ascension of Jesus is mentioned briefly here in the Gospel according to Mark, but most of the details we have about this event come from St. Luke, recorded in both his Gospel and again in the Acts of the Apostles (the first reading assigned for this weekend—Acts 1:1–11).

There are several biblical resonances within the Ascension story. Let's start with Luke's account of the Transfiguration. There we see Moses and Elijah speaking with Jesus about how he would depart from Jerusalem—his exodus (see Luke 9:29–31). The prophet Elijah was famously taken to heaven in a chariot of fire (2 Kings 2:1–12), and in the time of Jesus the Jewish faithful believed that Moses had similarly been assumed into heaven. From the final chapter of the Torah (Deuteronomy 34), they knew that Moses went up to Mount Nebo and was never seen again. An obvious editor recounts that he died and that God buried him on the mountain. In Jewish tradition. Joshua sent numerous search parties to find the body but never did. Over the next fifteen hundred years the Jewish "sense of the faithful" was that Moses—like Enoch before him (Genesis 5:24) and Elijah after him—was assumed into heaven. If God had done it before God could do it again. Luke writes at the end of his Gospel that Jesus is also assumed into heaven (Luke 24:50), and he opens Acts with the same story.

And so we come to our Gospel reading this week. It is taken from the "longer ending" of the Gospel of Mark, which most scholars see as having been editorially crafted from insights gleaned from the synoptic Gospels (Matthew, Mark, and Luke) and from Acts.

This set of summary verses allow for echoes of the Great Commission from the Gospel of Matthew (Matthew 28:18–20), the signs and wonders that accompany the apostles in their ministry in the Gospels and Acts, and Luke's account of the Ascension. We also see signs of the promised Holy Spirit and speaking in new tongues (see Acts 2:1–13). Finally, note the teaching that believers will be able to handle deadly serpents, which have resonances with St. Paul's experiences in Acts 28:1–6.

Emboldened by these events the disciples went out to proclaim the good news everywhere. We should still be about doing the same today.

Meditatio

Everything is different. The resurrected Lord has ascended into heaven and is seated in authority with God. It is the turning point in history. The victory of Jesus over the grave and the great commission he gives his apostles is now universal in scope. All humanity can be reconnected with God.

"Go into the whole world and proclaim the gospel to every creature." The message of the life, death, burial, and resurrection of Jesus is for all. A relationship with God is no longer limited to the geographic confines of Israel or to the Jewish people. The gospel message will move from Judea north to Samaria and then to Galilee and from there to Damascus, Antioch, and (by the end of the Book of Acts) to the very edges of the known world—the Roman Empire (Acts 1:8).

This message of salvation continues to expand. As disciples we participate in the advancement of the gospel in our own time. The commission has not changed. There are countless peoples who still need to hear the good news. They need to be offered the opportunity to be baptized and saved. We may be the only Bibles some people will ever read. Our gospel-themed lives can be a living witness of what it means to be saved—freed from the punishment of sin and restored to a right relationship with God. This is our calling as disciples. It moved the apostles outward in the past and will motivate us into service in the present.

Oratio

This prayer of St. Anthony of Padua serves well this week as we pray for the needed fortitude to go into all the world and proclaim the gospel: *O God, send your Holy Spirit into my heart that I may perceive, into my mind that I may remember, and into my soul that I may meditate. Inspire me to speak with piety, holiness, tenderness, and mercy. Teach, guide, and direct my thoughts and senses from beginning to end. Amen.*

Contemplatio

"And they went out and proclaimed the good news everywhere, while the Lord worked with them and confirmed the message …" (Mark 16:20 NRSV). The earliest disciples of Jesus hit the road with the saving message of the gospel. They went forward in the confidence that the Lord would work with them to confirm the message they were commissioned to deliver with signs and wonders. They stepped out in faith and trusted that the promised Holy Spirit would be there to assist them in this important work.

Today the call remains the same for you and me. We may not feel particularly ready or trained up enough to take the good news of Jesus into our world, but we are called to act in faith and get moving in the right direction. If our hearts are in the right place Jesus will supply whatever we lack for the journey. We are his eyes, we are his ears, and we are his voice in the world. We have to start sometime. We have to start somewhere. Why not here and now? Be the light of Christ to your world this week!

OTHER READINGS: ACTS 1:1–11; EPHESIANS 4:1–13

PENTECOST SUNDAY

THE MIGHTY ACTS OF GOD

ACTS 2:1–11

1 When the time for Pentecost was fulfilled, they were all in one place
together. 2 And suddenly there came from the sky a noise like a strong
driving wind, and it filled the entire house in which they were. 3 Then
there appeared to them tongues as of fire, which parted and came to
rest on each one of them. 4 And they were all filled with the holy Spirit
and began to speak in different tongues, as the Spirit enabled them
to proclaim.

5 Now there were devout Jews from every nation under heaven staying in Jerusalem. 6 At this sound, they gathered in a large crowd, but
they were confused because each one heard them speaking in his own

language. 7 They were astounded, and in amazement they asked, "Are
not all these people who are speaking Galileans? 8 Then how does each
of us hear them in his own native language? 9 We are Parthians, Medes,
and Elamites, inhabitants of Mesopotamia, Judea and Cappadocia,
Pontus and Asia, 10 Phrygia and Pamphylia, Egypt and the districts of
Libya near Cyrene, as well as travelers from Rome, 11 both Jews and
converts to Judaism, Cretans and Arabs, yet we hear them speaking in
our own tongues of the mighty acts of God."

Lectio

We anticipate celebrating the feast of Pentecost and so will focus on the first reading assigned for this week, from Acts 2. Fifty days have passed since the resurrection. Jesus has ascended into heaven and is seated at the right hand of the Father. He has directed the disciples to remain in Jerusalem until they are clothed with power from on high. Pentecost is that day of empowerment—the day God's promised Spirit descends upon those gathered in the upper room and the Spirit-inspired message of salvation will be proclaimed by Peter on the temple mount.

We share the feast of Pentecost with the Jewish faith community, who celebrate it to remember the giving of the law to Moses and the Israelites at Mount Sinai. Fifty days after the Israelites are liberated from Egypt they find themselves at the base of a mountain in the land of Midian (modern Saudi Arabia). There they receive the Ten Commandments and God makes a covenant with them that establishes their nation (Exodus 19–20). Pentecost (from the Greek word for fifty) is thus celebrated fifty days after Passover; Christians celebrate Pentecost fifty days after Easter.

In our reading we find all the disciples together one place, the upper room—probably the same room used by Jesus and the disciples to celebrate the Last Supper. Luke reports that 120 are gathered together, both men and women. The weather in Jerusalem features afternoon breezes, drawn from west to east in the late afternoon, settling into a calm by morning. This morning the typical quiet is interrupted by a sudden and violent wind, a microburst, that descends upon the upper city. The room is shaken by a wind that "filled the entire house."

Violent bursts of wind are rare here, and the noise catches the attention of the "devout Jews" who are in Jerusalem for the feast. These pilgrims have been heading to the temple for the morning sacrifice, but the microburst in the Upper City causes them to hurry to see what is happening. The gathering crowd witnesses the first miracle of "tongues"—a group of men and women, each filled with a new Spirit of God, all speaking at once, ecstatic in their praise of God and God's good deeds. The new arrivals are amazed. They have come from the most distant parts of the Roman Empire, but somehow each one is able to hear and understand in their own native language what the disciples are saying.

This Pentecost experience is evangelistic. The deeds of God are being proclaimed to pilgrims who have traveled great distances to be in Jerusalem for the feast. They will take this experience—and the gospel message—home with them after the feast. Paul reminds the church in Rome that "faith comes from what is heard" (Romans 10:17), and what these faithful people hear and understand in their own language are words of praise of God and thanksgiving for God's mighty works. They ask one another, "What does this mean?" (Acts 2:12). An answer is on the way.

Meditatio

"Amazed and astonished …" That is the reaction of the devout men and women who came from the temple mount to the upper room on the day of Pentecost. Drawn by curiosity and the witness of the mighty wind they arrive to find the earliest disciples of Jesus caught up in the expressions of God's wonders through the spiritual gift of tongues. When visitors arrive in our churches, are they "amazed and astonished" by what they see and hear? Is the Holy Spirit helping us to speak their native languages? What kind of evangelization would be possible if we were more open to the Holy Spirit working powerfully in our weekly gatherings and in our individual lives? Are we are afraid to be amazed and astonished ourselves? If this is true, we should pray for the courage to ask why.

In the Pentecost story those pilgrims who make their way across the city to the Upper Room witness the Holy Spirit speaking through the disciples and they cannot believe their own ears. They thought they knew these people—they were all Galileans, provincials. The pilgrims were the world travelers, skilled in speaking multiple languages. Why has God chosen these Galileans for the expression of this unique and fascinating gift of tongues? They ask the correct question in response to what they see and hear: "What does this mean?" The question is just as compelling today. What does this all mean?

Oratio

This prayer is a Pentecost standby but perfect for our preparation to celebrate the feast this week: "Come Holy Spirit and fill the hearts of your faithful and kindle in them the fire of your love. Send forth your Spirit and they shall be created. And you shall renew the face of the earth."

Contemplatio

In John 14:16 Jesus promises that he will ask the Father who will send "another Advocate," the Holy Spirit, to be with the disciples forever. Pentecost celebrates the fulfillment of that promise. Now, filled with the Holy Spirit, we are led by the Spirit as we follow the Lord. The Spirit appears in the Upper Room as "tongues of fire" that settle upon all present. Fire and light define the Christian experience. The first command in the Book of Genesis is "Let there be light!" The Gospel writer names Jesus as the "life [that] was the light of the human race." That light "shines in the darkness, and the darkness has not overcome it" (John 1:4–5). Jesus is still that light, and we are to be the flames he uses to draw the attention of others to himself. We should be willing to shine brightly for the Lord, to put our light on a lampstand so that it will give light to everyone in the room. I fondly recall singing "This Little Light of Mine" in Vacation Bible School: "This little light of mine, I'm going to let it shine, let it shine, let it shine!" Shine as a light in your world this week in the way that you love God and others.

OTHER READINGS: 1 CORINTHIANS 12:3b–7, 12–13; JOHN 20:19–23

BUT THEY DOUBTED

MATTHEW 28:16–20

> 16 The eleven disciples went to Galilee, to the mountain to which Jesus
> had ordered them. 17 When they saw him, they worshiped, but they
> doubted. 18 Then Jesus approached and said to them, "All power in
> heaven and on earth has been given to me. 19 Go, therefore, and make
> disciples of all nations, baptizing them in the name of the Father, and
> of the Son, and of the holy Spirit, 20 teaching them to observe all that
> I have commanded you. And behold, I am with you always, until the
> end of the age."

Lectio

Our Gospel this week is found in the last verses of Matthew, known as the Great Commission. Jesus had directed the eleven disciples (apostles) to meet him on "the mountain" in Galilee. "Eleven" reminds us that Judas is missing. Matthew refers to them as disciples because they are still "students" of Jesus during the forty days between his resurrection and ascension. Jesus will use this time to complete their formation. The likely location of this story is on the slopes of Mt. Hermon near the site of the transfiguration. Peter, James, and John would know the way since this was where they had witnessed Jesus "transfigured" in all his heavenly glory (Matthew 17). The eleven arrive ahead of Jesus and then the Lord appears.

Our Gospel author, Matthew, is an eyewitness. He records that when the disciples saw Jesus they worshiped him. "Worship" is the same word he uses to describe the response of the twelve after Jesus appeared to them walking on the waters (see Matthew 14:33). When Peter is called out of the boat to walk on the churning Sea of Galilee, Jesus had just identified himself to the disciples as "I AM" (Matthew 14:27), a name reserved for God and revealing to the disciples that he was divine. The disciples pay Jesus the honor he is due; they worship him as God in their midst.

Now Jesus reminds the eleven that all power in heaven and on earth has been given to him. He has conquered even death. The "one like a son of man" in Daniel's vision is promised similar power and authority by God and is invited to take his throne next to the Ancient of Days (Daniel 7:13–14). Since this universal power has been given to Jesus, he can give his disciples a universal mission. They are now sent to bring the message of the gospel to the nations, not just to the lost sheep in the house of Israel (Matthew 10:6, 15:24). The term "nations" refers to the Gentiles, all the people groups who are not Jews. All the nations are to be called to become disciples of Jesus, members in the new family of God, the church! New sisters and new brothers are on the way. That is the Great Commission. The disciples needed the final training so that they can continue Jesus's work in the world.

Meditatio

"When they saw him, they worshiped, but they doubted." What was going on in the minds of the eleven on that day? They greet the risen Lord in Galilee and worship him as a divine figure yet we see that doubt remains. What kind of doubt has crept into their minds as they made their way to the mountain rendezvous? Let's return to the scene on the Sea of Galilee in Matthew 14:22–33. Jesus appears to the disciples. He is walking on the water! He calls Peter out to him and he steps out of the boat! Peter is actually walking on the water, but then he begins to doubt. He begins to sink. Jesus saves him, takes him into the boat, and says to him, "O you of little faith, why did you doubt?"

I found that a bit harsh until I realized that Jesus is actually quite proud of Peter. He lacks only that last bit of faith, the aspect of complete trust that would have completed the third part needed for biblical faith. In one definition, for biblical faith to be present, you begin with knowledge, which is followed by belief (in the sense of assent or agreement), and then completed with trust (putting your weight on it). Peter was so close! He was almost there. Well done, Peter—you only lack the last aspect of biblical faith, trust. So trust and do not doubt. It is after this statement that the disciples in the boat pay Jesus homage—they worship him as God.

On the mountain the eleven still harbor doubt. Why did we lose Judas? What will happen next? How will we explain what we have experienced to our families? These concerns (and others) are considerable and quite normal. We, like the disciples of Jesus we meet in the New Testament, move forward in faith through stages. We begin with what we know and then progress to what we will believe. It is hard to get to the final stage, trusting our lives to what we know, but with the help of the Holy Spirit we can and will. The eleven who come down from the mountain that day know that Jesus has promised to be with them always, until the end of the age. He is still with his disciples—you and me—now.

Oratio

Pray the "Glory Be" in response to the Gospel reading this week. "Glory be to the Father, and to the Son, and to the Holy Spirit. As it was in the beginning, is now, and ever shall be, world without end. Amen."

Contemplatio

Jesus is challenging his disciples to move beyond the comfort of their nuclear and religious families of faith. They are going to become members of a new family that will eventually be called the church. In the Middle East "the other" is typically looked upon with suspicion. "They" are bad and "we" are good. We can make divides along lines of biology (race) or ethnicity (behavior). Jesus wants us to bridge those gaps and be ready to welcome all who respond to the gospel. Those who become disciples become our brothers and our sisters in Christ. Our common bond is our belief in a triune God. The Trinity, God in three persons bound by a single nature, binds Christians to each other no matter what race, family, or place we come from. We celebrate Trinity Sunday this week and recall that our God truly is with us still—and will be to the end of the age.

An action response to this Gospel could be to offer a special prayer for Christian missionaries of all traditions who are taking the message of salvation around the earth and making disciples of all the nations. Let's find a way to support them this week.

OTHER READINGS: DEUTERONOMY 4:32–34, 39–40; ROMANS 8:14–17

TAKE IT

MARK 14:12-16, 22-26

12 On the first day of the Feast of Unleavened Bread, when they sacrificed the Passover lamb, his disciples said to him, "Where do you want
us to go and prepare for you to eat the Passover?" 13 He sent two of his
disciples and said to them, "Go into the city and a man will meet you,
carrying a jar of water. Follow him. 14 Wherever he enters, say to the
master of the house, 'The Teacher says, "Where is my guest room where
I may eat the Passover with my disciples?"' 15 Then he will show you a
large upper room furnished and ready. Make the preparations for us
there." 16 The disciples then went off, entered the city, and found it just
as he had told them; and they prepared the Passover.

22 While they were eating, he took bread, said the blessing, broke it, and
gave it to them, and said, "Take it; this is my body." 23 Then he took a
cup, gave thanks, and gave it to them, and they all drank from it. 24 He
said to them, "This is my blood of the covenant, which will be shed for
many. 25 Amen, I say to you, I shall not drink again the fruit of the vine
until the day when I drink it new in the kingdom of God." 26 Then, after
singing a hymn, they went out to the Mount of Olives.

Lectio

This week we will celebrate Corpus Christi, the feast that remembers the Last Supper and directs our attention to the bread and wine that Jesus will reveal as his body and blood (Corpus Christi translates into English as the Body of Christ). Our reading finds Jesus and the disciples gathering to celebrate Passover. Jesus has carefully orchestrated the events that will culminate at this shared meal. He has arranged to have an upper guest room ready and directs the disciples to purchase food.

Jesus also engages in a bit of subterfuge. He directs the disciples to go to the city—to the pools of Bethesda, it seems, located just outside one of the northern gates of Jerusalem. There they are to look for a man carrying a water jar and follow him across the city to the guest room in the upper city where the Passover meal is to be prepared and later consumed. In biblical times woman were water carriers. Women carried water in jars carefully balanced on their heads or in a larger stone jar carried by two women. Men carried water in an animal-skin container slung under their arms and against their chest. A man carrying a water jar would be an anomaly. This fellow would be easy to spot and to follow across the city.

The Passover meal begins. Two ritual cups of wine (of four in the liturgy) have been consumed and the meal has been served. This is the third cup of the Passover, the Cup of Redemption that remembers God's deliverance of ancient Israel from slavery. Jesus interrupts the ritual meal when he offers the disciples bread and wine that he identifies as his body and his blood. He shifts the focus from the lamb they are eating to himself. Jesus is the new Passover lamb. In the old Passover rite the people must consume the lamb to conclude the sacrifice. This will also be true with Jesus and the new Passover. Jesus is the Lamb of God who has come to take away the sins of the world. This new Passover lamb must be consumed too.

Jesus promises the disciples that he will not drink wine again until he drinks it anew in the kingdom of God. Jesus and the disciples exit the Upper Room before the last cup of the Passover is consumed. The fourth and final cup of the Passover meal is called the Cup of Acceptance. This is the cup that Jesus refers to in the garden of Gethsemane. In Gethsemane Jesus will accept the will of the Father to lay down his life. The last public gesture of Jesus before he dies will be to consume the wine that is offered to him in his agony (Mark 15:36–38). This wine is consumed by Jesus at the same moment that the first official lamb is offered at the temple on that Friday afternoon. The Passover is complete. It has now been fulfilled in Jesus. He is the new Passover for us all.

Meditatio

Bread and wine. Jesus takes them and offers thanks to God for the blessing of both, and then he distributes these elements of the new Passover to the disciples. What is significant about bread and wine?

The bread of Passover is made without leaven. Leaven (yeast) is a raising agent that is added to dough in its preparation stage. Leaven is produced as a byproduct of decay. It smells terrible and would be kept hidden away in the darkest corner of the ancient kitchen until needed by the baker. At Passover you eat unleavened bread to avoid mixing things that are alive (wheat in the form of flour) with leaven, an agent of decay. This Passover bread is safe—we will not be made unclean by eating it. This is the bread Jesus offers to the apostles at the Last Supper.

Jesus also offers them wine. Wine is a spirit that can restore and refresh—and can also destroy the soul (Sirach 31:25–29). It is a dangerous "spirit" that must be consumed in moderation. Drinking wine is an important part of the Passover ritual. St. Paul counsels Timothy to drink more wine as an antidote to his many ailments (1 Timothy 5:23). But too much wine can be a problem and lead to serious health issues. Balance is the key. A little can go a long way.

This week take a moment to reflect on the different natures of the elements used by Jesus to reveal himself to us in every Mass. Bread and wine. One is safe and the other can be dangerous. Balancing the two is worth the risk. But what of us and our lives? Do we err on the side of safety and take no chances, or are we reckless in our spiritual adventures to the point that we risk our mortal souls? Balance is the key. Bread and wine. Safe and challenging at the same time.

Oratio

Before Jesus and the disciples leave the Upper Room they sing a hymn (Mark 14:26). The hymns sung at Passover are the "Hallel," Psalms 113–118. *Hallel* is a Hebrew word that translates as thanks. Jesus gave thanks and went out into the night. Let's pray a part of Psalm 116 this week. See if you can connect the Passion of our Lord to these verses.

"What shall I return to the Lord for all his bounty to me? I will lift up the cup of salvation and call upon the name of the Lord. I will pay my vows to the Lord in the presence of all his people. Precious in the sight of the Lord is the death of his faithful ones. O Lord, I am your servant … you have loosed my bonds. I will offer you a thanksgiving sacrifice and call on the name of the Lord." (Psalm 116:12–17 NRSV)

Contemplatio

Can you recite a psalm by memory? Perhaps this is how we can put our faith into practice this week. Do you best to commit one psalm to memory and build on that base in the weeks to come. Begin with Psalm 117. Psalm 117 is one of the Hallel Psalms and is the shortest of all the psalms collected in the Bible. Or how about Psalm 23? It is the perfect psalm to commit to memory. It can be recited with anyone in your life that you know and love, especially those who may be suffering or moving close to death. Psalm 23 brings comfort in those situations. Really, any Psalm will do. There is no wrong way to get started, so why not begin now? Memorizing Scripture is a wonderful spiritual practice that will help you grow in your faith.

OTHER READINGS: EXODUS 24:3–8; HEBREWS 9:11–15

TENTH SUNDAY IN ORDINARY TIME

OPPOSITION TO JESUS

MARK 3:20–35

20 He came home. Again [the] crowd gathered, making it impossible
for them even to eat. 21 When his relatives heard of this they set out to
seize him, for they said, "He is out of his mind." 22 The scribes who had
come from Jerusalem said, "He is possessed by Beelzebul," and "By the
prince of demons he drives out demons."

23 Summoning them, he began to speak to them in parables, "How can
Satan drive out Satan? 24 If a kingdom is divided against itself, that
kingdom cannot stand. 25 And if a house is divided against itself, that
house will not be able to stand. 26 And if Satan has risen up against
himself and is divided, he cannot stand; that is the end of him. 27 But
no one can enter a strong man's house to plunder his property unless he
first ties up the strong man. Then he can plunder his house. 28 Amen, I
say to you, all sins and all blasphemies that people utter will be forgiven
them. 29 But whoever blasphemes against the holy Spirit will never

> have forgiveness, but is guilty of an everlasting sin.” 30 For they had said,
> “He has an unclean spirit.”
>
> 31 His mother and his brothers arrived. Standing outside they sent word
> to him and called him. 32 A crowd seated around him told him, “Your
> mother and your brothers are outside asking for you.” 33 But he said
> to them in reply, “Who are my mother and brothers?” 34 And looking
> around at those seated in the circle he said, “Here are my mother and
> my brothers. 35 [For] whoever does the will of God is my brother and
> sister and mother.”

Lectio

“Home” for Jesus is Capernaum where he and his mother are hosted by Peter and Andrew and their extended family. This home has been the scene of numerous miracles and crowds have flocked to its doors trying to gain access to Jesus. Jesus has returned to Capernaum after a successful healing of a man who was both deaf and mute (see Matthew 12:22–37). Jesus restored both senses and then faced scathing criticism by some religious leaders, who insisted that Jesus had cast out the demons holding the man in their power by the power of demons themselves. They say that Jesus is possessed by Beelzebul, a demon agent of Satan, an enemy of God.

In Matthew’s account, those who witness the miracle originally wonder if Jesus is revealing himself as the Son of David, the promised Messiah. But others in the crowd follow the lead of the religious leaders and reject Jesus and this healing as the work of the devil. Tempers flare. Here, members of Jesus’s extended family arrive in Capernaum to “seize” him, arguing on his behalf that he is out of his mind. They want to save Jesus from himself! The energies emerging in opposition to him may be too much for Jesus to bear alone. They probably want to take him back to the safety of Nazareth. This protective gesture is well intentioned but misguided.

Now Jesus challenges the religious leaders and their negative assessment of the healing. Why, he asks, would Satan cast out demons from a man clearly in demonic clutches? If that were the case the religious leaders should celebrate and thank Jesus. He would be doing their job. Jesus notes that no kingdom divided against itself can stand for long, so if the religious leaders are to be believed the power of Satan will soon come to an end. Then Jesus takes a moment to explain what should be obvious: he is the stronger agent in this deliverance miracle. He was able to enter the strong man's house and plunder his property. He threw the strong man out and the victim's ability to speak and hear returned.

Jesus warns the assembled leaders that they may be guilty of "an everlasting sin," the one sin that cannot be forgiven. Jesus assures us that people can be forgiven for every sin and blasphemy. But these leaders sin by attributing the work of God to the enemy of God. They seem convinced that Jesus has an evil spirit within him and ignore all evidence to the contrary. They have made a mockery of God and his goodness displayed by Jesus's healing. This seems to be part of what Jesus means when he says they "blaspheme against the Holy Spirit."

Beyond this, their status and opinions as religious authorities will be honored by many in the crowd. Those who believe the warning that Jesus is an agent of Satan will be denied the opportunity to respond to the miracle in faith and recognize Jesus as he reveals himself as the promised Messiah. These leaders are blocking the path to salvation and will be held accountable. Like all religious leaders, they are held to a higher standard.

Meditatio

A beautiful moment brings this Gospel reading to a close. The mother of Jesus arrives on the scene and tries without success to enter the house due to the great number of disciples packed inside. Jesus is told that she is asking for him, and before he leaves the disciples (I assume here that he would honor her request to meet with him) he asks those seated around him who they think his mother and brothers are. There is no answer from the disciples, so Jesus answers his own question by saying that his mother and brothers are all those who do God's will. His mother Mary certainly fits that category. She said yes to the angel Gabriel and the plan of salvation was secured. When the assembled disciples say yes to Jesus they become members of the new family of faith that will become the church.

Who are your brother and sister and mother today? Take a few moments this week to recall and pray for those you might call your spiritual mothers, fathers, brothers, and sisters—those who have contributed to your faith in Jesus. Each of these is as much a mother or brother to you as an actual parent or sibling. Forty years ago a spiritual father to me, the Dominican Fr. Tom DeMan took me under his tutelage as a college freshman. Two years later I entered the novitiate in the Order of Preachers. A year later Fr. Tom witnessed my marriage to my wife Diane and later officiated at the baptisms of our children. He is as much a father to me as was my own dad, who also taught me what it meant to live a life of service to others by serving faithfully in our local parish. Who are your mother and fathers? Your sisters and brothers? Remember them this week and give thanks for the role that they have played (and will play) in your life of faith.

Oratio

Catholic Christians pray this prayer when they attend the Mass. We ask for and receive forgiveness so that we are ready to listen and respond to the Word of God. Pray it in anticipation of attending church this weekend.

I confess to almighty God, and to you, my brothers and sisters, that I have sinned through my own fault, in my thoughts and words, in what I have done, and in what I have failed to do; and I ask blessed Mary, ever virgin, and all the angels and saints, and you, my brothers and sisters to pray for me to the Lord our God. Amen.

Contemplatio

Jesus says that whoever does the will of God is his mother, his brother, his sister. How can we know when we are doing the will of God? How can we be sure? Our Jewish brothers and sisters offer us a unique insight into this challenge. It will be the subject of our contemplation this week.

For a Jewish person the challenge of finding the will of God is not tied up in trying to discover what God wants you to do. That is already clearly revealed in the Bible. The will of God is not a mystery to be solved. The question the Jewish person asks themselves is whether they will do the will of God, or not. The prophet Micah (6:8) reveals what the will of God is for every person of faith. "He has told you, O man, what is good; and what does the LORD require of you"—here comes God's will—"but to do justice, and to love tenderly, and to walk humbly with your God."

That's it! That is the will of God for you in every circumstance of your life. Now that you know what the will of God is, the next question becomes: will you do it? Will you live in these Micah principles? Ask yourself, "How can I be more just this week?" "How can I reveal God's tender mercy, God's kindness to others?" "How can I walk humbly with God this week?" In this new spiritual mindset we let go and allow God to direct our way. We place our God-given gifts and talents at the disposal of the Holy Spirit. These reflections will serve you well in the days to come.

OTHER READINGS: GENESIS 3:9–15; 2 CORINTHIANS 4:13—5:1

ELEVENTH SUNDAY IN ORDINARY TIME

SCATTERED SEED

MARK 4:26–34

26 He said, "This is how it is with the kingdom of God; it is as if a man
were to scatter seed on the land 27 and would sleep and rise night and
day and the seed would sprout and grow, he knows not how. 28 Of its
own accord the land yields fruit, first the blade, then the ear, then the
full grain in the ear. 29 And when the grain is ripe, he wields the sickle
at once, for the harvest has come."

30 He said, "To what shall we compare the kingdom of God, or what
parable can we use for it? 31 It is like a mustard seed that, when it is
sown in the ground, is the smallest of all the seeds on the earth. 32 But
once it is sown, it springs up and becomes the largest of plants and puts
forth large branches, so that the birds of the sky can dwell in its shade."
33 With many such parables he spoke the word to them as they were able
to understand it. 34 Without parables he did not speak to them, but to
his own disciples he explained everything in private.

Lectio

In the Gospel this week Jesus returns to the use of parables to reveal signs that promise the appearance of the kingdom of God (another way to translate *kingdom* is the "reign" of God). Jesus uses parables when teaching a large group of people, challenging the crowd to listen to his teaching in a new and meaningful way. His parables are stories drawn from nature and common life and always include some surprise to cause the audience to pause and reflect on what they have heard. They end abruptly and without explanation. Jesus wants to leave the listener in doubt as to a parable's precise meaning. He expects them to wrestle with the story and try to find its meaning for themselves. He always leaves the crowds wanting more. Jesus does explain the parables, but only in private and only to his disciples. The disciples will be expected to help others hear and understand.

In our first parable Jesus compares the kingdom of God with a farmer who scatters seed on the surface of the field and then ignores the rest of the practices expected of a farmer. In ancient Israel the farmer waited patiently for seasonal rains to arrive and soften the earth. After the soaking rains the farmer would cast seed on the field before plowing under as much as possible before the birds steal it all (see Mark 4:4). The farmer in the parable does not even bother to work the seed into the ground with the plow. It is left unattended. Jesus now reveals the surprise: The seed germinates, takes root, and produces a crop that can be harvested. That seed, representing the kingdom of God, had no chance at survival, but God takes over to produce an abundant harvest. What is Jesus teaching us?

In the second "kingdom of God" parable here we meet another farmer who is, for some reason, trying to seed his field with mustard. In the Middle East the mustard plant grows easily and is everywhere. The plant is a pest, and farmers do their best to eradicate mustard from their fields. But in the parable the farmer is sowing and plowing the seed into his field. That is our shock, the surprise that grabs and holds our attention. The small seed will grow quickly to become a bush large enough to choke off any other plants. It will take over the field. The reign of God will look like that. No one could see that coming!

Meditatio

The kingdom of God, the reign of God, is not an earthly monarchy but rather God's breaking forth into the world through the lives of those who believe. These two parables are stories of surprise and abundance. No one would give either crop a chance at survival. In the first parable the farmer does not follow appropriate protocols to ensure the seed will come to harvest. In the second parable the farmer is planting a seed that will grow into a plant every other farmer wants to eradicate. In both the seed takes root and grows to fruition. God even finds a way to make the common mustard bush useful. It will be suitable housing for the birds of the sky.

Jesus reveals a God of surprises, a God who does things you and I would never expect but that work out for our best in the end. "Whoever has ears ought to hear" (Matthew 11:15). This will be our challenge and our prayer this week.

Oratio

The parables in this week's Gospel reveal to us aspects of what the kingdom of God will be like. Let's lean again into the Lord's Prayer and the petition for that kingdom to be realized in our midst: *"Our Father in heaven, hallowed be your name; may your kingdom come, your will be done, on earth as in heaven."*

Contemplatio

The shock elements of Jesus's parables challenge the listener to a deeper understanding of faith. His parables are designed to get through to those who think they have heard it all before and are closed to new insights. The crowds needed a push to consider the work of God in a fresh way. We too need to be open to the shock, to the surprise of God working in our own lives this week.

Author Paula D'Arcy says that God comes to you disguised as your life! Sometimes we are so close to our own circumstances that we don't see the reign of God breaking through. Take a few moments to pray about how God has surprised you in the past. What do you remember about that experience now? Do you recall it fondly? Why? How did that God-inspired surprise change your life then? Does it still affect your life now?

OTHER READINGS: EZEKIEL 17:22–24; 2 CORINTHIANS 5:6–10

WHAT'S IN A NAME?

LUKE 1:57–66, 80

57 When the time arrived for Elizabeth to have her child she gave birth
to a son. 58 Her neighbors and relatives heard that the Lord had shown
his great mercy toward her, and they rejoiced with her. 59 When they
came on the eighth day to circumcise the child, they were going to
call him Zechariah after his father, 60 but his mother said in reply, "No.
He will be called John." 61 But they answered her, "There is no one
among your relatives who has this name." 62 So they made signs, asking
his father what he wished him to be called. 63 He asked for a tablet
and wrote, "John is his name," and all were amazed. 64 Immediately
his mouth was opened, his tongue freed, and he spoke blessing God.
65 Then fear came upon all their neighbors, and all these matters were
discussed throughout the hill country of Judea. 66 All who heard these
things took them to heart, saying, "What, then, will this child be?" For
surely the hand of the Lord was with him.

80 The child grew and became strong in spirit, and he was in the desert
until the day of his manifestation to Israel.

Lectio

The time arrives for Elizabeth to give birth to her son. He is the fruit of the promise made to her husband Zechariah while he was serving a priest in the holy place (see Luke 1:5–20). Zechariah doubted the word of God's angel and was struck dumb as a result. He is promised that his ability to speak will return upon the birth of the child. Although both are advanced in years, both will share the joy of parenting a son who will be the one to prepare the way of the Lord. Luke describes this couple as both "righteous in the eyes of God, observing all the commandments and ordinances of the Lord blamelessly" (verse 6). Because they had no children, they would have been considered less than righteous in the eyes of many in their village. God knows better, and because of Luke, so do we.

Who are the neighbors and relatives who now hear of the mercy God has bestowed upon Elizabeth and Zechariah? They are probably one and the same. In New Testament times the vast majority of persons who live in a village are related through birth or marriage. You would typically live the whole of your life in the same village and so would be well known to all. These relatives are ready to rejoice with Elizabeth because she has now been able to fulfill the commandment involving marriage, to be fruitful and multiply. In their world, children, children, and even more children are a direct sign of God's favor toward any married couple.

It would have been typical for Zechariah to announce the name of his son soon after his birth. The name would normally be that of the grandfather. The naming of this child is delayed until the eighth day of his life, the day of his circumcision. The village's plan was to break with protocol and name this son after his father Zechariah. To the shock of all assembled Elizabeth speaks for the couple (Zechariah is still mute) and announces that the child's name will be John. Her relatives kindly inform her that that is not the name of the child's grandfather or father. There is no history of that name in the family. They turn to Zechariah and offer him a tablet so that he can correct his wife's error in judgment. Zechariah agrees with Elizabeth and writes that the child name will be John. The relatives are amazed and Zechariah's tongue is loosed so that he can speak the praises of God. Everyone assembled that day knows that the Lord has big plans for John. They are sure that the hand of the Lord will be on him.

The reading ends by jumping thirty years into the future. John grows strong in the Lord and will become a prophetic fixture at the desert fording point along the Jordan River opposite Jericho. Soon his cousin Jesus will appear and will inaugurate his public ministry by submitting to baptism.

Meditatio

"All who heard these things took them to heart, saying, 'What, then, will this child be?'" In the Gospel of Luke both the neighbors and relatives in our reading and Mary the mother of Jesus "take things to heart." What does that mean? In the biblical world you do not process thought in your mind (as we do in our Western world) but rather the heart. The heart is the emotionally infused center of thought, prayer, and applied consideration. You meditate in your heart.

The villagers are intimately involved in the birth, circumcision, and naming of the son born to old Elizabeth and Zechariah. They have witnessed the miracle of the pregnancy, the birth, and now the public celebration making the child as a member of the Jewish faith community through the ritual of circumcision. They sense something special about this child given the unusual circumstances surrounding his conception and birth. He is a child of grace and a gift from God. They cannot know what all of this will mean, but they do know that the child is destined for great things in the service of the Lord.

Can you recall a time when you wondered what a child would become? With five young grandchildren, I am now revisiting these times of wonder all over again. I had an active hand in the formation of our five children but now I have to stand by and watch as my grown children, as parents, follow the Lord as they raise our grandchildren in our midst. What, then, will this child be? It is the question for our meditation this week.

Oratio

When Zechariah names his son with the name revealed by the angel Gabriel, his tongue is loosed and he begins to speak of the blessings of God. We can share in this blessing of the Lord in our prayer this week gleaned from the opening lines of Zechariah's inspired prayer in Luke 1:67–79. *"Blessed be the Lord, the God of Israel, for he has visited and brought redemption to his people"* (Luke 1:68).

Contemplatio

What is in a name? The son of promise born to Zechariah and Elizabeth should have had one of two names. Either the name of his grandfather or the name of his own father. Instead both parents insist that his name will be John, the name the angel Gabriel directed Zechariah to give his son. The name John comes from a Hebrew word that translates into English as "God is merciful" or "God has shown his favor." This is certainly the case for these new parents. Their son John is a sign of God's tender kindness and abounding mercy. What is the meaning of your name? How about your middle name? Do you know? The answer to this question is only a few keystrokes away. Ask the question for yourself this week. What does my name mean? Am I living out the meaning of my name? How has God shown me mercy and favor this week?

OTHER READINGS: ISAIAH 49:1–6; ACTS 13:22–26

THIRTEENTH SUNDAY IN ORDINARY TIME

YOUR FAITH HAS SAVED YOU

MARK 5:21–43

21 When Jesus had crossed again [in the boat] to the other side, a large crowd gathered around him, and he stayed close to the sea. 22 One of the synagogue officials, named Jairus, came forward. Seeing him he fell at his feet 23 and pleaded earnestly with him, saying, "My daughter is at the point of death. Please, come lay your hands on her that she may get well and live." 24 He went off with him, and a large crowd followed him and pressed upon him.

25 There was a woman afflicted with hemorrhages for twelve years. 26 She had suffered greatly at the hands of many doctors and had spent all that she had. Yet she was not helped but only grew worse. 27 She had heard about Jesus and came up behind him in the crowd and touched his cloak. 28 She said, "If I but touch his clothes, I shall be cured." 29 Immediately her flow of blood dried up. She felt in her body that she was healed of her affliction. 30 Jesus, aware at once that power had gone out from him, turned around in the crowd and asked, "Who has touched my clothes?" 31 But his disciples said to him, "You see how the crowd is pressing upon you, and yet you ask, 'Who touched me?'" 32 And he looked around to see who had done it. 33 The woman, realizing what had happened to her, approached in fear and trembling. She fell down before Jesus and told him the whole truth. 34 He said to her, "Daughter, your faith has saved you. Go in peace and be cured of your affliction."

35 While he was still speaking, people from the synagogue official's
house arrived and said, "Your daughter has died; why trouble the
teacher any longer?" 36 Disregarding the message that was reported,
Jesus said to the synagogue official, "Do not be afraid; just have faith."
37 He did not allow anyone to accompany him inside except Peter, James,
and John, the brother of James. 38 When they arrived at the house of
the synagogue official, he caught sight of a commotion, people weeping and wailing loudly. 39 So he went in and said to them, "Why this
commotion and weeping? The child is not dead but asleep." 40 And they
ridiculed him. Then he put them all out. He took along the child's father
and mother and those who were with him and entered the room where
the child was. 41 He took the child by the hand and said to her, "Talitha
koum," which means, "Little girl, I say to you, arise!" 42 The girl, a child
of twelve, arose immediately and walked around. [At that] they were
utterly astounded. 43 He gave strict orders that no one should know this
and said that she should be given something to eat.

Lectio

In the Gospel this week there is a healing story within a healing story. I would like to draw your attention to the healing of the woman suffering from a constant hemorrhage of blood, which happens as Jesus makes his way to the home of a local synagogue official.

Jesus arrives in Capernaum, his ministry headquarters. He is well known here as a healer, preacher, and teacher and is immediately surrounded by a large crowd. People press in on him from every side. He is informed that the daughter of the synagogue leader, Jairus, lies at home and is near death. Jesus agrees to accompany Jairus to his home where he will pray for his little daughter. Jesus "leads" the crowd from the center of the assembled disciples. In the Middle East a leader is surrounded by his followers. They are loyal to him and can protect him from any danger by acting as a human shield. Progress toward any destination is slow and deliberate. The crowd grows as they move closer to their destination.

On the way a nameless woman appears. She has hemorrhaged blood for the past twelve years. Mark notes that she has spent all she had on doctors but has only grown worse. Ancient doctors worked more like philosophers than like medical doctors in our time. They would much rather talk about a particular condition than lay hands on a patient and risk failure. Good advice would be given but not a cure. Your only other recourse would be an act of faith.

She approaches Jesus in the center of the crowd and does her best to "touch his clothes." Her intent is to grasp one of the four tassels (called *tzitzit)* that descend from each corner of his prayer garment, the *tallit* that Jewish men wear in obedience to a commandment in Numbers 15:38–39. This woman believed that the tassels of the Messiah would bring healing if grasped. This was a traditional teaching of Judaism in the time of Jesus, which also helps explain why Jesus has such a difficult time watching some religious leaders preen in public wearing the prayer shawl with "elongated tassels" (see Matthew 23:5–7)—they are suggesting to the general population that they might be the Messiah. Mark 6:56 describes this same act of faith: those who touch the tassels on the corners of Jesus's prayer shawl are healed!

When she grasps a corner tassel the progress of Jesus is halted. Jesus asks his disciples to find out who touched him. Looking around at the crowd, they wonder who hasn't! But Jesus knows that power has gone out of him and that the person who grasped the tassel acted in faith. He wants to identify her to honor her. She has believed Jesus is the Messiah and acted boldly on that belief when the opportunity presented itself. When she identifies herself to Jesus there is great joy among the crowd.

But one person in the scene does not share her joy. During the delay caused by this healing a report reaches Jesus and Jairus that his little daughter has died. Jesus immediately turns to the distraught Jairus and in a calming tone tells him not to be afraid. He must have faith. His faith in Jesus will be rewarded when his daughter is called back from the grave.

Meditatio

I am captivated by the emotions that Jairus must have experienced during his time with Jesus that day. His hopes must have soared when he heard that Jesus had returned to Capernaum. He finds him and asks for his help. Jesus agrees to come to his house to pray for his little girl who is wasting away in her room. Anthropologists estimate that 2000 years ago nearly 60 percent of children who survived birth died before they reached their teens. Could this be the fate of his sweet girl? Heaven forbid. Jairus comes to Jesus with faith in his ability to heal his daughter. Then a woman, a social outcast who cannot immediately be identified, brings the procession to his home to a standstill. What will be the cost of this delay? His impatience grows with each passing moment. The woman who was healed finally reveals herself (finally!) and Jesus begins again to move toward his home. Then the tragic news! His beloved daughter has died. There is no need to trouble the teacher any longer. All is lost. I can only imagine the face of Jairus as he looks at Jesus in disbelief and despair. His pleading eyes invite Jesus to say something. To do something. Anything!

The response of Jesus is swift and sure. He disregards the message. Don't listen to them! Jesus looks directly at Jairus and says, "Do not be afraid; just have faith." This outcast "daughter of Israel" has reached out in faith and was healed. She is his example. She has been figuratively "dead"—untouchable, for exactly the same number of years Jairus's daughter has been alive!—and now has been called back to life. Her faith saved her. Will the faith Jairus has in Jesus be enough to see his beloved daughter alive again? I cannot get the look of the face of Jairus out of my mind. The shock. The fear. The hope. The resignation that he will simply have to trust Jesus and enter the room where his little girl lies asleep in death, waiting for the call that will awaken her back to life.

Oratio

In the Gospel of Mark (Mark 9:14–25) Jesus meets a father with a son who desperately needs healing. Jesus says to the father he need only believe and his son will be healed. The response of this father to Jesus is our prayer this week. He cries out, "I do believe, help my unbelief!"

Contemplatio

Faith and action. The two go hand in hand. A traditional saying sometimes attributed to Saint Augustine is that Christians should pray as though everything depends on God and then work (act) as though everything depends upon you. This is demonstrated in this Gospel passage. The faith of Jairus and of the unnamed woman is revealed in their actions. The synagogue official finds Jesus and asks him to pray for his dying daughter. The woman reaches out in the faith that Jesus is the Messiah of Israel who can heal her if she could only grab hold of one of the tassels of his prayer shawl. Both are rewarded for their actions. Both reach out to Jesus and both find healing.

Where is the lesson for us? Our life of faith needs to be in concert with our actions. Sometimes we need to reach out and ask for help or healing. Pray for that boldness this week and be encouraged by the witness of Jairus and this beloved daughter of Israel that we met this week.

OTHER READINGS: WISDOM 1:13–15; 2:23–24; 2 CORINTHIANS 8:7, 9, 13–15

FOURTEENTH SUNDAY IN ORDINARY TIME

HIS NATIVE PLACE

MARK 6:1–6

> 1 He departed from there and came to his native place, accompanied by
> his disciples. 2 When the sabbath came he began to teach in the syna-
> gogue, and many who heard him were astonished. They said, "Where
> did this man get all this? What kind of wisdom has been given him?
> What mighty deeds are wrought by his hands! 3 Is he not the carpenter,
> the son of Mary, and the brother of James and Joses and Judas and
> Simon? And are not his sisters here with us?" And they took offense
> at him. 4 Jesus said to them, "A prophet is not without honor except in
> his native place and among his own kin and in his own house." 5 So he
> was not able to perform any mighty deed there, apart from curing a
> few sick people by laying his hands on them. 6 He was amazed at their
> lack of faith.
>
> He went around to the villages in the vicinity teaching.

Jesus returns to his "native place"—the hilltop village of Nazareth where he was raised. He is well-known in the village. He would have lived here from the time he was a young boy until he left at age thirty. Nazareth is located along a ridge high above the Jezreel Valley. In Jesus's day the village had a well-won reputation as a hotbed of political insurrection. The Romans who patrolled the Via Maris travel route along the base of the ridge did not pay much attention to Nazareth. Finding your way there required an arduous climb and any intention of surprise would be thwarted by lookouts who could follow your progress from a great distance.

The reputation of Nazareth as a politically charged and religiously zealous village is summed up by the apostle Nathaniel. Learning that his friend Philip thinks that the Messiah may be Jesus who is from Nazareth, Nathaniel responds by asking whether anything good can come from there (John 1:44–46). The insinuation is that if you associate with anyone from Nazareth you do so at your own risk. Those Nazareth hotheads are difficult to deal with and no friends to the Roman military occupation.

In his home village Jesus is called the "son of Mary." Typically in the Middle East a son is identified by the name of his father. Peter, for example, is called Simon bar John, Simon the son of John. Is our Gospel author Mark trying to hint at the mysteries surrounding the conception and birth of Jesus? That is possible. The village itself would have been populated by immediate and extended family members. Jesus is the adoptive son of Joseph, who is called a "carpenter," a term that may translate better into English as "contractor," someone who could work easily with many types of building materials. Stone is the most common in that area.

Jesus arrives in Nazareth riding a wave of success and support. News of his miraculous activities precedes his arrival. A hemorrhaging woman had been healed. The daughter of a synagogue leader had been called back from the grave. And at a wedding in nearby Cana he had performed a public miracle by transforming water to wine! His growing band of students accompany him from Capernaum and are gratified when Jesus is invited to read and comment on the prophet Isaiah that day (Luke 4:16–21). The villagers honor Jesus by offering this invitation to read and preach.

They all know Jesus and yet are stunned by the content and manner of his teaching. They wonder where he has discovered this authority and wisdom. Who has this friend of ours become since he left the village?

But then they take offense at him. Why? A possible explanation is found in the Middle Eastern concepts of honor and shame. Like everyone in this culture, Jesus was given an "ascribed" honor status at birth. He is and will be what his father and mother are and have always been in Nazareth. But Jesus has surpassed his ascribed status. Maintaining your status quo is the norm, but Jesus breaks that barrier and rises to unprecedented heights. Everyone in the synagogue wonders how this has happened. They know his family members. The offense they take toward Jesus may be rooted in the fact that he seems to think more highly of himself than he should. They want to bring him down a notch or two.

Jesus is amazed at their lack of faith. This word used in the New Testament conveys the concept of loyalty. Those in the synagogue that day were members of his own family. He expected more support.

Meditatio

Jesus is amazed at the lack of faith he found among those he knew best, his immediate and extended family members. The Greek word that translates as brother and sister refers to a much larger group than biological siblings. The "brethren" of Jesus have lived in Nazareth the whole of their lives and thought they knew Jesus. Then he went away and has returned a transformed man. There is a difference in Jesus now. He teaches with a new authority that amazes everyone in the synagogue.

Before his return they had heard the stories of his miracles. They had to be impressed by the large group of students that have accompanied him to his home village. Why can't they respond well to this "son of Mary"? Why do they take offense at him that day? Whatever the reason Jesus is amazed. Imagine the pain of Jesus in this scene. He is rejected in the synagogue by those people who know and love him most. He wants to heal and bless but he cannot because of their growing animosity. It was a hard day to come home, and Jesus leaves Nazareth, never to return.

Oratio

Take a moment this week to offer prayer for all the members of your family who were part of your "native place." Ask the Lord to remind you of all of the extended family who contributed to your growth in the Lord and to your life in the faith. You will be pleasantly surprised whom the Lord will call to your memory. When each name comes up, pray for them this week.

Contemplatio

Where is your "native place"? Where are you from? Are people there who remember you from the days that you grew up together? Do you still live there? When was the last time you visited? If you can't visit, when is the last time that you called someone from your "native place" to catch up or just say hello? Maybe this would be a good week to get back in touch. Visit the old homestead. Call your mom or your dad. Reconnect with siblings or cousins. Too much time has passed. Take the initiative to connect and enjoy the fruit of a good visit or lively conversation.

OTHER READINGS: EZEKIEL 2:2–5; 2 CORINTHIANS 12:7–10

FIFTEENTH SUNDAY IN ORDINARY TIME

AUTHORITY AND REPENTANCE

MARK 6:7–13

[7] He summoned the Twelve and began to send them out two by two
and gave them authority over unclean spirits. [8] He instructed them to
take nothing for the journey but a walking stick—no food, no sack, no
money in their belts. [9] They were, however, to wear sandals but not a
second tunic. [10] He said to them, "Wherever you enter a house, stay
there until you leave from there. [11] Whatever place does not welcome
you or listen to you, leave there and shake the dust off your feet in
testimony against them." [12] So they went off and preached repentance.
[13] They drove out many demons, and they anointed with oil many who
were sick and cured them.

Lectio

In the Gospel this week we find Jesus sending the Twelve on an internship. He commissions them for a short practicum to heal and preach in his name in the nearby villages in advance of his own arrival. Jesus sends them out two by two. This is likely done for safety as well as for the consolation of companionship in ministry. Travel is dangerous in New Testament times—especially if you travel alone. Recall that in the parable of the Good Samaritan the lone traveler is assaulted by bandits and left for dead.

It is not to be a lengthy internship. They are to take only the bare necessities. They will not need extra funds or an additional coat because they will not be gone long enough to experience a change in the seasons, though they can wear sandals, the normative footwear in the period.

The Twelve can expect to be welcomed in the villages they enter. They will arrive as strangers in villages made up of extended family members. Hospitality is expected in the Middle East. One reason hospitality is offered to any stranger is as a means of discerning whether they are friend or foe. The preparation and presentation of food takes time and is an opportunity for conversation. Your hosts will find out as much as they can about you before the meal is served. Failure to extend hospitality is a serious breach of honor; a guest would treat this as a major insult and would not leave the village without addressing it in a public manner. Thus Jesus instructs the Twelve that if they do not receive the hospitality normally accorded to a stranger, they are to leave the village and slap their sandals together, a symbolic gesture that brings shame on the village population, announcing that you do not want even the dust of its streets to leave with you on this day.

The apostles are to heal and preach in the name of Jesus. The ministry of Jesus is carefully orchestrated—usually healing, preaching, and then teaching. Here the Twelve are seen healing and driving out demons—which draws a large crowd—and preaching, stirring people's hearts to repentance. Jesus will follow up later, arriving in the village to teach more about the kingdom of God. The Twelve are not yet ready to teach. This final part of their commission will come to them at the end of the public ministry of Jesus.

Meditatio

What does Mark mean when he mentions Jesus giving the Twelve "authority over" unclean spirits? In the biblical world spiritual beings were ranked by perceived power, with God at the apex of the hierarchy. Authority may be delegated, and Jesus is God's agent, exercising all God's authority! Then come the archangels (traditionally seven in all) followed in ranks by various orders of angels and demons. St. Paul speaks of these as "principalities" and "powers" and "evil spirits in the heavens" (Ephesians 6:12). Humans were ranked lower. Here Jesus elevates the honor status of the Twelve a full level. They can now cast out demons by the authority given them by Jesus.

In his letter to the Philippian church St. Paul writes that at the name of Jesus every knee will bend, whether in heaven, on the earth, or even under the earth (Philippians 2:10). There is power in the name of Jesus as much in our time as in New Testament times. Sit quietly with the name of Jesus on your mind and in your heart as you prepare to worship this weekend.

Oratio

There is power in the name of Jesus. One ancient prayer deeply rooted in Scripture is used in quiet meditation and contemplation among our Eastern Christian sisters and brothers. It is called the Jesus prayer. This simple prayer is recited over and over with each intake and exhalation of a breath. It calms the soul and feeds the spirit. Practice this prayer form this week: *"Lord Jesus Christ, Son of the living God, have mercy on me, a sinner."*

Contemplatio

Mark tells us that the apostles "preached repentance" in the villages and towns of Galilee. The word repent originates in a Greek word that conveys turning around so you can come back to where you were before. When John the Baptist invites people to repent he is calling those who have crossed the Jordan River on their way to Jerusalem to stop, turn around, and come to him so that they can listen to his message. They are invited to come back so they can hear what he has to say. The apostles are sent to preach this same message of repentance. They are inviting people to stop, turn, and listen to the good news that Jesus is proclaiming in Galilee.

We too need to hear the invitation to repent. There are times when we need to be invited back to hear the message of the gospel afresh. It might mean returning to a church. It might mean returning to a relationship. It might mean slowing down enough to hear the voice of the Lord in the gentle whisper of the breeze. The preaching of repentance is not harsh. It is an invitation to come back, to get to know the Lord in a new way—now, today. Listen for that invitation and respond in kind this week.

OTHER READINGS: AMOS 7:12–15; EPHESIANS 1:3–14

SIXTEENTH SUNDAY IN ORDINARY TIME

COME AWAY

MARK 6:30–34

30 The apostles gathered together with Jesus and reported all they had
done and taught. 31 He said to them, "Come away by yourselves to a
deserted place and rest a while." People were coming and going in great
numbers, and they had no opportunity even to eat. 32 So they went
off in the boat by themselves to a deserted place. 33 People saw them
leaving and many came to know about it. They hastened there on foot
from all the towns and arrived at the place before them.

34 When he disembarked and saw the vast crowd, his heart was moved
with pity for them, for they were like sheep without a shepherd; and he
began to teach them many things.

Lectio

The internship is over and the apostles have returned to Jesus in Capernaum. They brim with excitement as they share the fruit of their efforts to heal and preach his message of repentance in the towns and villages in Galilee. They are not alone. Word of their success has reached the ears of many and great numbers of people have followed them home. The crowds are so overwhelming that they cannot even eat a meal.

In the world of the Middle East meals are communal and leisurely. Guests are always welcome. No matter their numbers, the host is expected to provide hospitality for them all—including bread, wine, and engaging conversation while the principal meal is prepared. Here with so many people in town there is no chance that Jesus or anyone else can host such a large group. Their only recourse is to leave Capernaum by boat and cross the lake to find "a deserted place" on the other side of the lake. The term refers to uninhabited land in between the many small villages of a particular area. Jesus would often cast demons into deserted places. In our passage, his intention is to take the apostles away from the pressing crowds. No one would be likely to follow and so place themselves in peril.

Capernaum is a fishing town on the northwestern shore of the Sea of Galilee. The commercial fishing grounds are located across the lake in the northeastern quadrant, near the village of Bethsaida. A careful study of the Gospels suggests that six of the twelve apostles were from this single village. Crossing the lake to these fishing grounds is quite easy in the afternoon given the prevailing westerly breezes. When Jesus and the apostles take to the water heading east, the Capernaum crowds know exactly where they are going. There is a well-worn path around the north of the lake. On foot—and Mark notes that they traveled with haste—they will arrive in Bethsaida before Jesus and the others.

Jesus and the apostles arrive to find the crowds waiting on the shore. Jesus feels pity for them. They are like sheep who have wandered to this remote location without a shepherd. They are ready. It is time for him to teach them and this he will do until the late afternoon sun dips toward the horizon.

Meditatio

Jesus sees a vast crowd assembled. In the Gospel account we read that he has pity on them. This word in Greek is often rendered as "compassion." It corresponds to a Hebrew word that means "bowels" or "womb," the source of deep emotions in the biblical world. Jesus is conveying a maternal expression of care and concern for the multitudes. The heart of Jesus goes out to those who appear before him like sheep without a shepherd. His compassionate love is revealed in this powerful word.

Why are the crowds described as being like sheep without a shepherd? Sheep in a flock need to be directed by the shepherd or they will simply lie down and refuse to fend for themselves. Without a shepherd they are in danger. They need the tender care of the rod and staff to protect them and guide them along "paths of righteousness." Mark is recording the preaching of the apostle Peter in this Gospel. Peter remembers the loving heart of Jesus revealed in the way he related to the expectant crowds that day. He would not leave them. He would teach them how to live in a way that would please the Father.

Oratio

The crowds were so motivated to know more about the kingdom of God that multitudes were inspired to drop everything and make their way with haste to find Jesus in a deserted place. That sort of drive is the source of our prayer response this week, taken from Psalm 42:1–3. Pray that you will have the same desire this week. *"As the deer longs for streams of water, so my soul longs for you, O God. My soul thirsts for God, the living God."*

Contemplatio

What would it take for you to plan and invite good friends over for a leisurely meal this week? We are all accustomed to our "fast food" lifestyle. We rarely gather together around a table with good friends and family members. Jesus wanted just such a meal with the apostles. They had just returned from a successful ministry internship but could not find time to tell their stories because of the crowds. What is your excuse? What keeps you from planning a meal-themed gathering in your home, unconnected to any holiday? This might be a real call to action in response to our desire to sit and share a leisurely meal with those that we love, to listen to their stories about how God is working in their lives. Bon Appetit!

OTHER READINGS: JEREMIAH 23:1–6; EPHESIANS 2:13–18

SEVENTEENTH SUNDAY IN ORDINARY TIME

MORE THAN FOOD

JOHN 6:1–15

1 After this, Jesus went across the Sea of Galilee. 2 A large crowd followed him, because they saw the signs he was performing on the sick.
3 Jesus went up on the mountain, and there he sat down with his disciples. 4 The Jewish feast of Passover was near. 5 When Jesus raised his
eyes and saw that a large crowd was coming to him, he said to Philip,
"Where can we buy enough food for them to eat?" 6 He said this to
test him, because he himself knew what he was going to do. 7 Philip
answered him, "Two hundred days' wages worth of food would not
be enough for each of them to have a little." 8 One of his disciples,
Andrew, the brother of Simon Peter, said to him, 9 "There is a boy here
who has five barley loaves and two fish; but what good are these for so
many?" 10 Jesus said, "Have the people recline." Now there was a great
deal of grass in that place. So the men reclined, about five thousand
in number. 11 Then Jesus took the loaves, gave thanks, and distributed
them to those who were reclining, and also as much of the fish as they
wanted. 12 When they had had their fill, he said to his disciples, "Gather
the fragments left over, so that nothing will be wasted." 13 So they collected them, and filled twelve wicker baskets with fragments from the
five barley loaves that had been more than they could eat. 14 When the
people saw the sign he had done, they said, "This is truly the Prophet,
the one who is to come into the world." 15 Since Jesus knew that they
were going to come and carry him off to make him king, he withdrew
again to the mountain alone.

Lectio

The apostles' internship has come to an end and they join Jesus in Capernaum to share their joy. Growing crowds are drawn to the village, so numerous that there is no place for quiet reflection. They cannot even eat a meal in peace! We saw last week that Jesus decides the best course of action is to get into boats and sail eastward, across the Sea of Galilee to a deserted location near the fishing village of Bethsaida.

John tells his readers that the feast of Passover is near. It is springtime. The barley harvest has been completed and the hillsides are covered with a blanket of new grass. Jesus and the apostles arrive on the eastern shore and are greeted by a huge crowd of men, women, and children. The crowd has come by foot and waits anxiously for Jesus to appear in hopes that he will continue his ministry of healing. In the parallel accounts of the same story in the synoptic Gospels, Jesus greets the huge crowd and then sits down to teach them. At the end of his teaching the disciples approach Jesus, suggesting that he dismiss the crowd so that they can return to their homes and an evening meal before the sun sets. John, by contrast, focuses our attention on Jesus's initiative.

Jesus sees that the people are weary and hungry after their long journey. He wants to feed them. He turns to Philip, an apostle who was raised in nearby Bethsaida. Philip insists it cannot be done. Two hundred days of wages—two thirds of an annual average salary—would not be enough to buy each member of the crowd even a single bite. How many are present in this scene? The Greek word used here for "men" denotes a male between the age of twenty and fifty. There were most certainly younger and older men present, in addition to the women. The number who need to be fed is closer to ten thousand than five.

Jesus is provided with five barley loaves, each the size of an average dinner roll, and two fish. Fish sourced from the Sea of Galilee might here have been cured, pickled, salted, or dried. In any case the food is not enough to feed even one person. Jesus takes these gifts and offers thanks to God for them before directing the disciples to distribute the food to the seated crowd. The food is multiplied so effectively that all eat and have their fill. Twelve baskets full of bread are left over! (These baskets came from the commercial fishing boat used to bring Jesus and the apostles across the lake. They had been stacked neatly in the vessel for use with each evening's catch. As the fish were drawn from the lake in nets, the marketable fish were tossed into these waiting baskets.)

The crowds are amazed. The miracle of multiplication has a Moses-like quality. It reminds them of the provision of manna during the years of wilderness wandering. They wonder aloud if "the Prophet" has appeared in Galilee. This is a reference to Deuteronomy 18:15 where Moses promises that another Prophet, one like himself, will one day appear. That Prophet was understood as the promised Messiah. Is Jesus this new Moses? He has to withdraw from the crowds to avoid them making him their king by force. Political insurrection is not part of the Father's plan. Jesus dismisses both crowds and apostles and retires to a lonely place to pray.

Meditatio

The crowd that greeted Jesus and the apostles that day made their way spontaneously from Capernaum. There was no planning, no preparation. They hungered for more than food; they hungered to follow Jesus. He was the healer, the preacher, the teacher they had been waiting for all their lives. They dropped what they were doing and hurried to make sure they would arrive in Bethsaida before he sailed into port.

Where is that hunger in our lives? What do you hunger for? Healing? A deeper relationship with the Lord? Spiritual intimacy? What would it take to motivate you to drop everything and find your way to a gathering of believers? A church mission? A particular service? With no money, no provision, no plan? That is the same motivation that inspired the thousands who found their way to Jesus that day. Were they expecting a miracle of multiplication? I can't imagine so, but they were amazed to experience it. I wonder what it was like to witness the multiplication.

Reserve a few moments this week to put yourself in the scene and see if you can feel the wonder of that day. The crowds respond in faith and proclaim that the Prophet has appeared. Messiah has come!

Oratio

Jesus "gave thanks" before he broke the provided loaves and fish and began to distribute them to the crowd. The prayer Jesus prayed is well known in Jewish tradition. We can tap into this prayer this week. Use this prayer in preparation for sharing a meal with family and friends: *"Blessed are you, Lord our God, King of the Universe, by whose word all things came to be."*

Our God is a God of multiplication. What can we bring to the Lord this week in hopes of our gift being multiplied? Take a moment to think about three things—your time, your talents, and your treasure. Each of these can be offered to the Lord in the expectation that what you bring to God will be multiplied.

Look closely at your weekly schedule. Where can you show up this week to help at church or in a ministry of outreach? That would be a way of offering your time to the Lord. What talent can you bring to the cause that the Lord can use as a multiplier of blessing? You can always find an opportunity to serve if you open your heart to the Lord. The Lord has gifted you with particular talents that can be multiplied in their expression. If you can't be present in person you can still make a financial contribution to a ministry. That is a way to share your treasure with the Lord. You can provide funds that will be multiplied in the service of those in need. Return to the Lord what you have been given and watch the blessings flow.

OTHER READINGS: 2 KINGS 4:42–44; EPHESIANS 4:1–6

EIGHTEENTH SUNDAY IN ORDINARY TIME

BREAD ALWAYS

JOHN 6:24–35

[24] When the crowd saw that neither Jesus nor his disciples were there,
they themselves got into boats and came to Capernaum looking for
Jesus. [25] And when they found him across the sea they said to him,
"Rabbi, when did you get here?" [26] Jesus answered them and said,
"Amen, amen, I say to you, you are looking for me not because you saw
signs but because you ate the loaves and were filled. [27] Do not work for
food that perishes but for the food that endures for eternal life, which
the Son of Man will give you. For on him the Father, God, has set his
seal." [28] So they said to him, "What can we do to accomplish the works

of God?" 29 Jesus answered and said to them, "This is the work of God,
that you believe in the one he sent." 30 So they said to him, "What sign
can you do, that we may see and believe in you? What can you do?
31 Our ancestors ate manna in the desert, as it is written:

'He gave them bread from heaven to eat.'"

32 So Jesus said to them, "Amen, amen, I say to you, it was not Moses
who gave the bread from heaven; my Father gives you the true bread
from heaven. 33 For the bread of God is that which comes down from
heaven and gives life to the world."

34 So they said to him, "Sir, give us this bread always." 35 Jesus said to
them, "I am the bread of life; whoever comes to me will never hunger,
and whoever believes in me will never thirst."

Lectio

Our Gospel opens the day after the multiplication miracle near Bethsaida. Jesus and his disciples are back across the lake in Capernaum. Jesus will preach a sermon in the local synagogue that will later be known as the Bread of Life Discourse. We are reading half of it this week.

People from distant villages have made their way to Capernaum. They are intrigued by Jesus and want to know more about his miraculous powers. The day before Jesus was compelled to dismiss many of these same people so that he could retire to a lonely place to pray. These are the folks who proclaimed Jesus as the Prophet, another title for the Messiah promised by Moses in Deuteronomy 18:15–18. They were ready to make Jesus king by the force of a public announcement, but he had more work to do on the other side of the lake. Now they find Jesus again, anticipating another miracle. Jewish tradition taught that when Messiah appeared he would reveal himself to be a new Moses, and like Moses would once again provide bread from heaven (the manna of Exodus 16). Discussions during the course of the previous evening must have convinced many that Jesus is that promised one of God.

Jesus addresses the growing crowd. He is impressed that they are willing to travel so far to find him, that they have worked so hard rowing their boats across the Sea of Galilee in the hope that he would again provide bread for them to eat. Jesus reminds them that any physical bread he could provide, like the manna of old, would eventually perish with mold and decay. He tells them to seek "the food that endures for eternal life."

Jesus does reveal himself as Messiah to those assembled that day, referring to himself as the Son of Man, a Messianic title drawn from Daniel's vision in Daniel 7:13–14. They immediately put a question to him: What can they do to find approval from God? The answer is simple. They are to believe in the one that God has sent. The Greek word that translates *believe* means not just intellectual assent but also loyalty and trust. To please God they need to trust in Jesus and remain loyal to him.

The crowd wants more. They want another sign. Moses called down the manna from heaven. He also had a staff that contained a serpent and was God's agent during the casting of the ten plagues on the Egyptians. What can Jesus do to top that? The manna in the wilderness stopped once their ancestors entered the Promised Land. The proof they demand is that Jesus provide them with bread that never runs out.

This week's reading concludes with Jesus's acknowledgment of their request. He tells them "I am the bread of life." The most challenging part of the sermon is about to begin.

Meditatio

Food is a powerful motivator—especially food that is free and abundant. Yesterday bread and fish had been multiplied. Everyone ate their fill and still twelve baskets full of bread remained. A new form of manna had appeared, but now Jesus could not be found. Men and women, young and old, people from every walk of life get into boats and amble along paths to find Jesus. They seek him so that he will feed them again—and feed them he will, but this time with a new bread, which he calls the bread of life. This teaching will change the way they relate to him forever.

Put yourself in one of the homes to which the crowd scatters after experiencing the multiplication miracle. Imagine the conversations of those evening hours. They had all experienced the miracle—manna from heaven had appeared again! Messiah will bring "bread from

Heaven"—could Jesus of Nazareth be the Messiah of God after all? The conversations lead to a plan. We need to ask him more questions. But where is he now? Where did he and his disciples go? Their boats were heading toward Capernaum as the sun was setting. In the morning we will go there and find him. This is not the end, this is the beginning of something wonderful.

Oratio

The Lord's Prayer includes an appeal for God to give us our "daily bread." For the Jewish audience in the Gospel this petition would recall the manna in the wilderness, a miraculous provision from the beginning to the end of their forty years of wandering in the wilderness. Keep this thought in mind as you pray the Lord's Prayer this week.

Our Father in heaven, hallowed be your name, your kingdom come, your will be done, on earth as it is in heaven. Give us today our daily bread—the bread of life—and forgive us our debts, as we forgive our debtors.

Contemplatio

This week our call to action is a call to faith. Jesus tells us that the work of God is believing in the one he sent. To believe is to act. We show we believe when we are loyal to Jesus and live our lives according to his teaching. All acts of faith, including all the corporal works of mercy, any acts of service to others, or even simply attending our local church events, reveal the level of loyalty and trust we have in Jesus. Our lives become the barometer of our faith.

Belief is so much more than just intellectual assent. That is often where it begins, but faith has to be lived. Be aware of the opportunities to witness about Jesus in the way you live your life this week. Make the most of every opportunity to shine your light so that all can see you belong to Lord!

OTHER READINGS: EXODUS 16:2–4, 12–15; EPHESIANS 4:17, 20–24

BREAD FROM HEAVEN

JOHN 6:41–51

> 41 The Jews murmured about him because he said, “I am the bread that
> came down from heaven,” 42 and they said, “Is this not Jesus, the son of
> Joseph? Do we not know his father and mother? Then how can he say,
> ‘I have come down from heaven’?” 43 Jesus answered and said to them,
> “Stop murmuring among yourselves. 44 No one can come to me unless
> the Father who sent me draw him, and I will raise him on the last day.
> 45 It is written in the prophets:
>
> ‘They shall all be taught by God.’
>
> Everyone who listens to my Father and learns from him comes to me.
> 46 Not that anyone has seen the Father except the one who is from God;
> he has seen the Father. 47 Amen, amen, I say to you, whoever believes
> has eternal life. 48 I am the bread of life. 49 Your ancestors ate the manna
> in the desert, but they died; 50 this is the bread that comes down from
> heaven so that one may eat it and not die. 51 I am the living bread that
> came down from heaven; whoever eats this bread will live forever; and
> the bread that I will give is my flesh for the life of the world.”

Our Gospel begins where we left off last week. Jesus is in the midst of delivering a sermon on the bread of life in the synagogue of Capernaum the day after he had miraculously multiplied bread and fish and fed the multitudes. This miracle inspired many to come to Capernaum in search of Jesus. Most believed that Jesus was the Prophet, God’s promised Messiah, who had appeared in Galilee with a new form of manna (the bread from heaven) in his wake. To fully appreciate the sermon and the exchange in the synagogue we need to listen with Jewish ears. Jesus captivates and challenges his audience with every word he speaks that day!

We find the Jewish crowd arguing about what Jesus means by saying he is “the bread that came down from heaven.” They would have heard in this a clear claim to divine status. Their biblical scholars had thought hard about the miraculous provision of manna in Exodus. Rabbinic authorities of the age taught that the manna that sustained the Israelites in the wilderness had been created by angels before the creation of Adam and Eve (Psalm 78:25). More manna was now reserved in heaven and would be returned to the earth with the coming of Messiah. So they protest. How can Jesus and the "bread from heaven" be the same? They know him and his parents well. This claim borders on blasphemy.

Jesus challenges his listeners to stop "murmuring" among themselves. Why the two-time use of murmuring? The word is chosen by our Gospel writer to recall the murmuring of the Israelites just before God provided the original "bread of angels" in the wilderness (Exodus 16:2, 7–8).

Jesus knows people. Even his disciples are going to be challenged by this teaching, and so he says that no one can come to him unless they are drawn to him by the Father. Jesus quotes the promise of Isaiah that "They shall all be taught by God" (Isaiah 54:13). He is referring to a vision of the New Zion when Messiah will appear and all will made new. In that age to come, everyone will be "taught by God"—and that seems to be what is happening in the synagogue this very day.

Jesus shocks those listening again when he declares himself the bread of life. And then he calls himself "the living bread that came down from heaven"! Their ancestors ate the manna in the wilderness, but eventually they all died anyway. Jesus says he is the living bread that has come down from heaven. He will also have to be consumed, but how? Jesus promises that whoever eats this bread (his body) will live forever, and additionally that this bread is his flesh that will be given for the life of the world. There are more shocks to come. The most difficult part of this teaching will be revealed in next week's Gospel.

Meditatio

Jesus knows his teaching on the bread of life is controversial. He knows he will be challenged at every turn. He is making the bold claim he is the Messiah. He is sent from God. He is the bread of life. He has seen the Father. Whoever eats the bread of his flesh will live forever. Live forever?

Where have we heard that phrase before in the biblical narrative? The first time eternal life is promised for consuming something is in the book of Genesis. Our first parents were expelled from the garden of Eden before they could eat of the fruit that would impart eternal life (Genesis 3:22–23). Now that food has returned. Jesus says *he* is the bread of life. But we know him. We know where he is from. We know his parents. How can he be the Messiah? But … he fed the multitudes, the sick are healed, and the good news is proclaimed to the poor.

Do the words of Jesus still challenge us in the same way? Is he the Messiah or just another religious teacher, one of many with insight into the human condition? Jesus is speaking to Jewish people in a Jewish way, but the challenge is the same for every Christian. Is Jesus who he claims to be—the virgin-born, sinless son of God and our savior—or not? Where do you stand? What do you believe? Where are you today? Remember that no one can come to Jesus unless the Father draws him. How have you been drawn to Jesus in your life? What is your unique story of faith? We each have our own story and every story is compelling. Think about how God drew you to Jesus as you prepare to hear the Gospel proclaimed this week.

Oratio

Bread is a simple and basic form of nourishment. Daily bread sustains us so that we can live the life God intends. In our prayer this week we should be even more attentive of our need for that bread that comes down from heaven. This bread might be in the form of the elements offered on the altar or in insights we receive in our quiet time with God in his Word. In either case we can pray: *Our Father in heaven … your name is holy. May your kingdom come and your will be done on earth as it is in heaven, and give us this day our daily bread.*

Contemplatio

Jesus makes a promise to those in the synagogue of Capernaum that everyone who listens to his Father and learns from him comes to Jesus. How does that work? How do we listen to the Father? Where does the Father teach us about the Son? In the Word. The Bible (especially the Old Testament) is a record of God speaking to people of faith over the course of generations. Those books, from Genesis to Malachi, all continue to speak about Jesus if you have the spiritual eyes to see. You will discover this message when you the take the time to read the Word. Rededicate yourself to a systematic reading of the Bible. Open your heart and experience for yourself the Father speaking to you through the Word. You will be drawn to Jesus too.

OTHER READINGS: 1 KINGS 19:4–8; EPHESIANS 4:30—5:2

TWENTIETH SUNDAY IN ORDINARY TIME

THE NEW MANNA

JOHN 6:51–58

> 51 "I am the living bread that came down from heaven; whoever eats
> this bread will live forever; and the bread that I will give is my flesh for
> the life of the world."
>
> 52 The Jews quarreled among themselves, saying, "How can this man
> give us [his] flesh to eat?" 53 Jesus said to them, "Amen, amen, I say to
> you, unless you eat the flesh of the Son of Man and drink his blood,
> you do not have life within you. 54 Whoever eats my flesh and drinks
> my blood has eternal life, and I will raise him on the last day. 55 For
> my flesh is true food, and my blood is true drink. 56 Whoever eats my
> flesh and drinks my blood remains in me and I in him. 57 Just as the
> living Father sent me and I have life because of the Father, so also the
> one who feeds on me will have life because of me. 58 This is the bread
> that came down from heaven. Unlike your ancestors who ate and still
> died, whoever eats this bread will live forever."

Lectio

This week we dive into the heart of the sermon Jesus delivers in Capernaum the day after the feeding of the five thousand. Jesus is making a bold declaration to the gathered crowd: he is the "living bread" that has come down from heaven.

We saw last week that the rabbinic sages believed that the manna God provided to sustain the Israelites in the wilderness was present in heaven before the creation of the world and would return with the Messiah when he appeared. Jesus thus claims to be Messiah when he says he has come down from heaven. He has brought with him "the bread of the angels" (Psalm 78:25) as evidence of his divine status. But Jesus is just getting warmed up! The teaching that follows will drive a wedge between him and some of the disciples, as Jesus now equates the bread from heaven with his flesh that he will give for the life of the world.

In the synagogue the response is immediate. A quarrel breaks out. How can Jesus give us his flesh to eat? That would amount to cannibalism. In fact, the Greek word that comes out in our translation as "flesh" seems carefully chosen to unsettle them. The word is *sarx,* and it refers to the actual flesh that is stripped off an animal. This is the kind of flesh Jesus says his disciples must consume if they want to inherit eternal life.

Can Jesus be speaking symbolically? His hearers cannot think so. Manna is not symbolic. It was real, collected and consumed by the people daily for almost forty years. They placed a golden vessel filled with manna in the tabernacle next to the Ten Commandments (Exodus 16:32–34). The new manna Jesus speaks about must be greater than the original. If the original was literal, even more so the new manna.

In the face of the quarrel, Jesus does not back down. He repeats and underscores this teaching. His disciples will have to eat the flesh of the Son of Man (a title for the Messiah from Daniel 7:13) *and* drink his blood if they want to have his life within them. His flesh is true food and his blood is true drink. The particulars of how the body and blood of Jesus are to be consumed are not yet revealed, but the teaching is clear: the body and blood of Jesus have to be consumed to attain eternal life.

This is blasphemy to many in the synagogue. There are strict prohibitions against both in the Law. How could any of this please the Father? Confusion reigns in the chamber. No one has ever taught like this before, or since! Jesus knows this. He reminds the skeptics that their ancestors ate the original manna—and they all died. This new manna from heaven will be food that will sustain the disciples until they experience eternal life.

Meditatio

We should take a moment to consider the character of the original manna as we continue to meditate on this challenging teaching. What was the provision of manna all about? God sent the first manna to sustain the Israelites during their forty years of desert wandering. It was miraculous from beginning to end. It was to be collected daily and would not keep for longer than twenty-four hours. But on Friday morning you were to collect twice as much, to feed your family over the Sabbath. Friday's manna would last forty-eight hours! Moses directs Aaron to collect a vessel full of the manna and place it in the ark of the covenant, and God promises that the manna collected in that golden vessel would remain fresh forever as a constant reminder of God's generous provision and care.

Now take a moment to meditate on the new bread that has come down from heaven. This new must surpass the old just as the Old Testament prefigures the New and the New Testament fulfills the Old. If Jesus is the new manna, he too is both miraculously present and divinely provided. The old manna sustained the Israelites but eventually ended. The new manna, the body and blood of Jesus, is present now and will remain with his followers until the end of time. The Old Testament manna ceased when the Israelites crossed into the Promised Land. The provision of the new manna, the body of Jesus, will cease when we cross into eternal life. That is why Jesus promises us that when we eat this bread we can know we will live forever.

Oratio

I adapted this prayer from the website *Faith and Worship.* It captures the hope that we have in Jesus, the bread of life:

When the journey is long and we hunger and thirst, Bread of Life, sustain us. When the road is hard and our bodies weak, Bread of Life, heal us. When our spirits are low and we can't carry on, Bread of Life, revive us. When the challenge is great and the workers are few, Bread of Life, empower us. And when the victory is won and we see your face, Bread of Life, you will rejoice with us. Amen.

Contemplatio

Our challenge this week is to pay special attention to the liturgy's Eucharistic prayers, where we learn how Jesus eventually revealed himself to the apostles at the Last Supper. The Eucharistic prayers are drawn explicitly from Scripture. Find your way to 1 Corinthians 11:23–26. Read this passage with the knowledge that this teaching was written to the Corinthian church in AD 52! The tradition St. Paul passed on here predates the Gospel accounts recorded in Matthew, Mark, and Luke. At the Last Supper we learn how Jesus will give us his body and blood as true food and drink. The story is still being told two thousand years later and is as compelling now as it was in the time of our Lord.

OTHER READINGS: PROVERBS 9:1–6; EPHESIANS 5:15–20

TWENTY-FIRST SUNDAY IN ORDINARY TIME

THIS SAYING IS HARD

JOHN 6:60–69

60 Then many of his disciples who were listening said, "This saying is hard;
who can accept it?" 61 Since Jesus knew that his disciples were murmuring about this, he said to them, "Does this shock you? 62 What if you were
to see the Son of Man ascending to where he was before? 63 It is the spirit
that gives life, while the flesh is of no avail. The words I have spoken to
you are spirit and life. 64 But there are some of you who do not believe."
Jesus knew from the beginning the ones who would not believe and the
one who would betray him. 65 And he said, "For this reason I have told
you that no one can come to me unless it is granted him by my Father."

66 As a result of this, many [of] his disciples returned to their former way
of life and no longer accompanied him. 67 Jesus then said to the Twelve,
"Do you also want to leave?" 68 Simon Peter answered him, "Master, to
whom shall we go? You have the words of eternal life. 69 We have come
to believe and are convinced that you are the Holy One of God."

Lectio

This is the last of our four weeks with Jesus's long sermon known as the "bread of life discourse." It is unique to the Gospel of John, and our writer tell us that "many" of the disciples of Jesus, men and women who have become his students over the past few months, are at a loss. They call this teaching "hard" and wonder openly who can accept it. The word in Greek we translate as "hard" comes from the same root as "scandalous." This teaching of Jesus is scandalous and borders on blasphemy. Jesus has gone too far for them. If these followers take Jesus at his literal word they have to imagine some sort of cannibalistic ritual in the making. They have had enough and express their intent to leave his fellowship.

Jesus is well aware of the conflict he has engendered. He acknowledges the shock of his teaching and then doubles down with an even bolder set of claims. He wonders if these disciples understand the divine nature of his origins. What if they saw Jesus, the Son of Man (Jewish shorthand for Messiah) ascend to where he was before? It is likely that Peter, James, and John are in the synagogue that same day. These three disciples witnessed Jesus transfigured into a divine figure outside Caesarea Philippi.

Jesus says that it is the spirit that gives life, but they are thinking according to the flesh. They lack the spiritual eyes they need to understand this teaching. This is not just symbolic. In John 4:24, Jesus teaches the disciples that God is Spirit. God and Spirit are synonymous and are as real to Jesus as anything we can touch. Mere earthly thinking about this teaching will not lead anyone to a complete understanding of how to eat his body and drink his blood. Thinking according to the flesh, without the insight of the Spirit, will get you nowhere.

Many of his disciples leave the fellowship. Jesus doesn't chase after them. He is more concerned about the Twelve. The apostles have been with him from the beginning. If any of them were to leave it would be particularly painful. Peter answers for the others with an assurance of their loyalty. "To whom shall we go? You have the words of eternal life." They do not fully understand the implications of this teaching but they are loyal to Jesus and will stay with him as long as they can.

Meditatio

"For this reason I have told you that no one can come to me unless it is granted him by my Father." This bold statement includes all of us who call ourselves Christians today. Because of this teaching we can be assured that our decision to follow the Lord is the result of grace and nature coming together into a perfectly timed invitation. God's grace abounds in supply sufficient to draw all men and women to faith, but not all who experience this grace will respond immediately. That is part of the mystery of faith.

Take a few moments this week to recall what God did in your life to prepare you in advance to respond to the call to faith when it came. What were the circumstances of the call? Who were the principle players? What had God done in your life to bring you to the point that you could finally say yes to the Spirit and this outpouring of grace?

Your faith is not an accident. The response you made to follow Jesus was a moment when you finally opened yourself up to the plan that God had for your life all along. If we have come to Jesus it is because this gift has been granted to us by the Father. The invitation was made and we responded. Give thanks for that this week.

Oratio

Lord, your words are Spirit and life. Give me the gift of courage to listen and respond to your Word so that I can grow in my faith, grow in my loyalty, and grow in my commitment to you as the Holy One of God, my Lord and Savior.

Contemplatio

Is there anything about Christian faith or teaching that you find "hard" or scandalous? It is easy to understand the decisions of friends or family who leave a particular Christian fellowship over a moral failure or public scandal. But the disciples in this week's Gospel leave because of a teaching they do not fully understand. Hopefully, some of them later return.

Do any parts of the Christian message challenge you like the Bread of Life discourse challenged the disciples that day? Does it offend you that Jesus teaches us to turn the other cheek? Do you struggle with the scandal of the cross? What about the doctrine of the Real Presence? Does the limitless mercy of God rub you the wrong way? Take a few moments to consider your "line in the sand" issues. I love the response of Peter. He is loyal almost to a fault. He doesn't understand this teaching, but he has seen enough to trust Jesus to fill in the blanks. We need to stand with Peter and assure the Lord that we also are convinced that Jesus is the Holy One of God. That is our call to action this week.

OTHER READINGS: JOSHUA 24:1–2a, 15–17, 18b; EPHESIANS 5:21–32

TWENTY-SECOND SUNDAY IN ORDINARY TIME

THE INSULTS OF JESUS

MARK 7:1–8, 14–15, 21–23

1 Now when the Pharisees with some scribes who had come from Jerusalem gathered around him, 2 they observed that some of his disciples
ate their meals with unclean, that is, unwashed, hands. 3 (For the Pharisees and, in fact, all Jews, do not eat without carefully washing their
hands, keeping the tradition of the elders. 4 And on coming from the
marketplace they do not eat without purifying themselves. And there
are many other things that they have traditionally observed, the purification of cups and jugs and kettles.) 5 So the Pharisees and scribes
questioned him, "Why do your disciples not follow the tradition of
the elders but instead eat a meal with unclean hands?" 6 He responded,
"Well did Isaiah prophesy about you hypocrites, as it is written:

'This people honors me with their lips,
but their hearts are far from me;
7 In vain do they worship me,
teaching as doctrines human precepts.'

8 You disregard God's commandment but cling to human tradition."

14 He summoned the crowd again and said to them, "Hear me, all of
you, and understand. 15 Nothing that enters one from outside can defile
that person; but the things that come out from within are what defile."

[21] "From within people, from their hearts, come evil thoughts, unchastity, theft, murder, [22] adultery, greed, malice, deceit, licentiousness, envy, blasphemy, arrogance, folly. [23] All these evils come from within and they defile."

Lectio

As Jesus's public ministry of healing, preaching, and teaching expands in Galilee it draws the attention of certain Pharisees and scribes. These religious leaders are willing to journey more than one hundred miles from Jerusalem. Arriving, they become upset that Jesus and his followers do not observe the strict interpretation of the Jewish law known as "the tradition of the elders" (verses 3–4). This code of conduct for everyday life had developed to ensure ritual purity in accordance with the Law of Moses.

Most of the disciples at this point are peasants from around Galilee, Jews in these rural areas had adapted the tradition of the elders to their rural setting. The Jerusalem leaders profess concern about the way they wash their hands before meals (the Hebrew word for hand is *yad,* and it refers to the whole arm from the tip of your longest finger to the point of your elbow). The disciples are not thorough enough, so their master must have taught them poorly. This is the basis for their challenge to Jesus.

Cultural life in the world of the Middle East revolves largely on retaining or gaining honor and avoiding the possibility of shame. In such a culture, any public question is a challenge to your honor. Leaving a question unanswered or being forced into a lie is a shameful loss of status, and the challenger will gain that lost honor for themselves. Each challenge must end with a winner and a loser. But Jesus is far cleverer than these religious professionals. When they question him, he sets them on their heels with an insult! Jesus calls them hypocrites—the Greek word also translates as *stage actor.* These respectable religious leaders say all the right words, but everyone knows they are only playing a part for the audience.

Jesus is not done yet. He continues by reciting from memory an applicable portion of Scripture from the prophet Isaiah about those who honor God only with their lips but not with their hearts—and so worship God in vain. People like this have lost their spiritual focus by placing human traditions, as helpful as they can be, before God himself. Then the final blow. Jesus says that these Pharisees and scribes have even abandoned the commandments of God to pursue human traditions.

They started the conflict when they challenged Jesus in this public forum. Jesus ends it with his rapid-fire staccato responses as he heaps shame after shame upon his opponents. Has Jesus won the day? It appears so because he then addresses the assembled crowds. Had he lost, they would not listen to any additional teaching.

Meditatio

As a practicing Catholic Christian, I have much in common with the religious leadership in the time of Jesus, especially in following "the tradition of the elders." By the time of Jesus that had been handed down from generation to generation for over fifteen hundred years. My community of faith has handed down a similar tradition for the last two thousand! I want to take a few moments to consider if my expressions of faith ever get in the way of loving God and living according to the Bible's teaching. I hope not.

It is easy for me to get carried away with proper procedure and protocol. My communion of faith is full of them—the sign of the cross, genuflection, standing on cue, reverent bows, the sign of peace, kneeling, receiving Communion in the hand or on the tongue. It is easy to get distracted by the pursuit of correct practice and potentially lose sight of God in the process. All of the above are important, but they pale in comparison to being born again and living as a child of God in a world darkened by sin. We need to find a spiritual balance in our lives so that we can serve God with our hearts and our hands, and also with our minds and actions.

Oratio

Two Scriptures come to mind as a prayer response to the Gospel reading this week. The first is found in the Sermon on the Mount. "Blessed are the clean of heart, for they will see God" (Matthew 5:8).

And: "Make every effort to live in peace with everyone and to be holy; without holiness no one will see the Lord." (Hebrews 12:14 NIV)

Keep both in mind as you prepare to worship this week. Pray for a pure and holy heart that will allow us to see the Lord in yourself and in others.

Contemplatio

What are the chances that I am a hypocrite? Jesus uses this word to describe the behavior of many religious leaders in his time. It conveys his frustration with their "acting" like men of faith in the public square. They had their script memorized. The words on their lips sounded wonderful but their hearts were far from God. I wonder if I too am sometimes just an actor on stage, going through the motions, doing all the right things with my heart far from God. If you share this same sense, we have to ask how we can break out of this condition. We need to find balance between our faith's forms and its doctrines. Human traditions are important and lead us toward God in public worship, but when we place these traditions before the doctrine, the divine revelation of God revealed in the Bible, it is easy to lose our way. We miss the forest if we are caught up focusing on a single tree. We must find the way to honor God with our lips and with our lives at the same time. It is the challenge of the Gospel this week.

OTHER READINGS: DEUTERONOMY 4:1–2, 6–8; JAMES 1:17–18, 21b–22, 27

TWENTY-THIRD SUNDAY IN ORDINARY TIME

BE OPENED

MARK 7:31–37

[31] Again he left the district of Tyre and went by way of Sidon to the Sea
of Galilee, into the district of the Decapolis. [32] And people brought
to him a deaf man who had a speech impediment and begged him
to lay his hand on him. [33] He took him off by himself away from the
crowd. He put his finger into the man's ears and, spitting, touched his
tongue; [34] then he looked up to heaven and groaned, and said to him,
"Ephphatha!" (that is, "Be opened!") [35] And [immediately] the man's
ears were opened, his speech impediment was removed, and he spoke
plainly. [36] He ordered them not to tell anyone. But the more he ordered
them not to, the more they proclaimed it. [37] They were exceedingly

> astonished and they said, "He has done all things well. He makes the deaf hear and [the] mute speak."

Jesus has just returned from his only excursion outside the land of Israel during his public ministry. After a brief stay in the region of Tyre and Sidon (along the coast of modern-day Lebanon) Jesus and his disciples return to Galilee by an unusual route that takes them across the top of the Sea of Galilee into the largely Gentile region known as the Decapolis. It was in one of the "ten cities" that Jesus recently cast out the legion of demons that had possessed a man (Mark 5:1–20). That man was sent to announce to his family what had happened to him. Could this be the reason for the return to the Decapolis cities? Perhaps.

Jesus's reputation as a healer precedes him. Now people bring to him a man who is not only deaf but also challenged in his ability to speak. Local "physicians" at the time were known for their ability to diagnose the condition of any patient but would rarely venture to lay a hand on their patients for fear they might not be healed. But Jesus is recognized as a healer who is not afraid to touch, manipulate, and speak authoritative words in bringing restoration of health to many. In this instance, the man's friends beg Jesus to act. We will never know why they needed to beg, but the fact that they persisted suggests that Jesus might have been otherwise occupied. I like to think that he was anxious to visit with the man from the Decapolis whom he had healed previously.

Breaking with his normal pattern of healing when approached in public, Jesus memorably pulls the deaf man aside and physically manipulates his ears and tongue—signaling to the man what is to come. Mark even records in the original Aramaic the words used to effect the healing. His deep, groaning sigh (read breath) commands that the ears and the mouth of this man "Be opened!" The man is healed. Immediately. He can hear and now speaks clearly.

Many witness the miracle, and Jesus commands onlookers not to tell anyone what they have seen. The problem is that the more he does so, the more they keep talking about the miracle and his methods. Why does the crowd disregard this direct command of Jesus to keep the event a secret? Is it because they live in the Decapolis and are therefore less religious than other Jews in Israel? Are they simply disobedient? Can our knowledge of the cultural world of the Middle East shed any light on the problem?

Actually, we know of a way of spreading a message that works uniquely well in the Middle East. In the West when asked to keep a secret we typically do our best to honor the request. In the Middle East, if a secret is shared with you, it means you are deemed honorable enough to share the news with others! With everyone you know. With everyone you meet! It becomes a commission to tell everyone!

Do you remember when Jesus tells his disciples that what they hear whispered in the inner room they are to proclaim from the rooftops (Matthew 10:27)? If you are honored by someone to know a secret, you are seen as worthy to announce it to others (see also Matthew 13:11). Even in our culture, we pay more attention when someone tells us they know "the secret of" life or happiness or peace.

This grapevine message technology serves the Middle East well. Seen this way, the command of Jesus is a commission to tell as many people as you can about the healing power of Jesus from Nazareth.

In Isaiah 35, the prophet imagines what the world will be like in the time of the Messiah. He writes boldly about the joys of the redeemed, when parched lands will flow with water so abundant that hidden crocus flowers will burst into bloom. The land will be blessed with the splendor of Carmel and Sharon—which means that the stately trees of Lebanon will reach toward the heavens as far south as Israel. In that time the faithful are encouraged to be strong and stand against any fear, because God will come with vengeance that will save and restore the land to the people of Israel. Isaiah proclaims that when God intervenes in human history you will know your salvation is near. How? Because in the time that follows this season of blessing, "the eyes of the blind [will] be opened and the ears of the deaf unstopped. Then will the lame leap like a deer, and the mute tongue shout for joy." (Isaiah 35:1–6 NIV)

These verses could have been on the mind of those in the crowd that day. Jesus had restored a man's hearing and speech with a single authoritative command. This man was known to them. They could attest that he was deaf and mute. Now they hear him singing the praises of God! "He has done everything well," they exclaim. In the immediacy of the moment the crowd recognizes that the time of Messiah has come. The messianic promises of Isaiah 35 are coming to pass. It is no wonder they are overwhelmed with amazement. But are we? How are we spiritually deaf and mute? How can our spiritual ears and tongue be opened this week? What would that look like? Give that some thought this week.

Oratio

We should pray with a renewed sense of thanksgiving and fervor like the man who had his hearing and voice restored in the Gospel. Two verses from the Psalms can guide us in our prayer.

Psalm 51:15: "Lord, open my lips, and my mouth will proclaim your praise."

Psalm 92:1–2: "It is good to give thanks to the Lord, to make music to your name, O Most High, to proclaim your love in the morning and your truth in the watches of the night!"

Contemplatio

"Ephphatha!" This one-word command in Aramaic translates into English as "Be opened." What do we need to open in our lives? Does our spiritual sight need to be restored? Ephphatha! Does our spiritual sense of hearing need to be tuned toward God and the Word? Ephphatha! Do our hands need to be opened so that we can use them in service to others? Ephphatha! And what about our wallets? Do they need to be opened so that many good works, good deeds done in the name and for the honor of God, can continue? Ephphatha! Open your hearts this week and let the Spirit speak to you. Remember to be open!

OTHER READINGS: ISAIAH 35:4–7a; JAMES 2:1–5

WHO DO PEOPLE SAY THAT I AM?

MARK 8:27–35

27 Now Jesus and his disciples set out for the villages of Caesarea Philippi.
Along the way he asked his disciples, "Who do people say that I am?"
28 They said in reply, "John the Baptist, others Elijah, still others one of
the prophets." 29 And he asked them, "But who do you say that I am?"
Peter said to him in reply, "You are the Messiah." 30 Then he warned
them not to tell anyone about him.

31 He began to teach them that the Son of Man must suffer greatly and
be rejected by the elders, the chief priests, and the scribes, and be killed,
and rise after three days. 32 He spoke this openly. Then Peter took him
aside and began to rebuke him. 33 At this he turned around and, looking at his disciples, rebuked Peter and said, "Get behind me, Satan. You
are thinking not as God does, but as human beings do."

34 He summoned the crowd with his disciples and said to them, "Whoever wishes to come after me must deny himself, take up his cross, and
follow me. 35 For whoever wishes to save his life will lose it, but whoever
loses his life for my sake and that of the gospel will save it."

Lectio

Our Gospel opens with Jesus and his disciples on the way to Caesarea Philippi, a Roman cultic center thirty miles north of Capernaum. It will take them the better part of two days to arrive. There they will see one of the three sources of the Jordan River, a mysterious cave that is considered a portal to the netherworld. They will marvel at the temple to Asclepius, the god of healing, and will wonder about the practices of those who come to Caesarea Philippi to worship Pan, the half-man half-goat trickster god. Jesus is confident that his followers will not be unduly influenced by the pagan surroundings. He has chosen this site, in the shadow Mount Hermon, to reveal to his apostles the first of his three passion predictions.

Most travel in the time of Jesus is done in groups. You are safer traveling with others and you can pass the time in conversation. As Jesus nears this journey's end he asks his disciples who the people they are traveling among say he is. He learns that the general response is favorable. He is compared with John the Baptist and any number of other prophets, including the great prophet Elijah. Jesus likes what he hears and issues no directive to correct this honorable assessment.

Then Jesus wonders about who he is to his most intimate followers. Peter, speaking as leader of the twelve, confidently responds that, based on their experiences with Jesus as a healer, preacher, and teacher, Jesus is the Christ, the Messiah of Israel, the promised "anointed one" sent from God. Jesus is happy to hear their assessment and directs them not to tell anyone in Caesarea Philippi this news. His honor status is already high, so the additional claim that he is the Messiah might upset the local population and hinder Jesus in what he intends to teach the apostles about what "Messiah" means.

They arrive in the bustling mountainside village and Jesus shocks the disciples with a new teaching that predicts his suffering, rejection by the elders, execution, and eventual return from the grave. The apostles listen in amazement. This won't happen on their watch! Peter pulls Jesus aside, intending to rebuke him for saying such things in a public forum. Jesus turns the tables, returning the rebuke with a stinging rebuttal. He calls Peter "Satan," which translated means that Peter has become an adversary who is trying to stop him from doing the will of the Father. Peter is crestfallen. He hears Jesus say, "Get behind me, Satan!" Out of my sight. Out of my way. I have work to do that you and the others cannot yet understand.

Jesus turns to those in his company to remind them that to be his follower requires the denial of the self and the acceptance of suffering, in this case, the cross! Peter will struggle with this teaching for the rest of the public ministry. He will defend Jesus as he is arrested in the garden by drawing a sword and shedding blood. He will accompany Jesus to his trial and wait outside in the dark courtyard for it to conclude. He will even deny he knows Jesus. Peter will also be the first apostle to enter the empty tomb on the day of the Resurrection. His uncertain journey of faith has only just begun.

Meditatio

"Who do people say that I am?" I am reminded of the famous argument of C. S. Lewis that there are finally only three choices available to a person considering the unique claims Jesus makes about himself. They are that Jesus is either the Lord, a lunatic, or a liar. Lewis suggests that Jesus would be a lunatic if he thinks he is God but is not—such a Jesus would be like a person who introduced themselves to you as a "poached egg." Jesus would be a liar if he knows he is not God's promised Messiah but presents himself as such. This would be a grand deception. Finally, Lewis asks if Jesus could in fact be who he claims to be, Lord and Messiah. If so, we owe him our honor, praise, and allegiance.

The question of Jesus in the Gospel is also personal. "Who do *you* say that I am?" How do you answer when Jesus asks this of you? Get to the root of your relationship with the Lord. It is natural to chart the growth over time that adds to our understanding of who Jesus is and how our relationship has changed over the years. Who was Jesus to you when your journey began? Can you put it into words? Who is he now? How have you grown in understanding? Who has helped you in this ongoing process? These are valuable meditative reflections to consider this week.

Oratio

Christian author John Piper notes that to deny ourselves in order to take up the cross means at least that we are willing to be opposed, to be shamed, to suffer, and even to be ready to die as a consequence of our allegiance to Jesus. We are called to treasure Jesus more that we treasure human approval, honor, comfort, and life itself.

Lord, give me the strength I need to lay down my life for you and what is yours. If this means bearing a cross, then give me the strength I will need to carry that burden in a way that will honor you and the Father. Amen.

Contemplatio

Who do people say that you are? We walk as followers of Christ in a world that needs to know Jesus. What do the others in your life know about your faith and its daily expression? Jesus teaches us that it is by our love for one another that the world will know we are his disciples (John 13:35). How is that witness coming along in your world? When people meet you, do they know that they are meeting a believer, a follower of Jesus?

Allow me to share an example from my life. I love to golf, which is an inherently social endeavor. On the tee, on the course, and on the green, I always try my best to be polite, supportive, and encouraging. I do not use language that would offend others as I want to project my best self to those in my company. On the green I mark my ball with a token that displays a cross and wait for the opportunity that typically arises when someone asks me about the marker and what it signifies. Am I a minister? A priest? What's my story? That's my opening to share my faith. I still pray for one woman, Val, who noticed the marker and concluded from that and my behavior that I must be a Christian. She was undergoing cancer treatments and asked me to pray for her whenever I use my ball marker. Who would she say that I am? A kind and considerate follower of Jesus, I hope. Pray for an opportunity to share your faith this week.

OTHER READINGS: ISAIAH 50:4–9a; JAMES 2:14–18

TWENTY-FIFTH SUNDAY IN ORDINARY TIME

AFRAID TO QUESTION HIM

MARK 9:30–37

> [30] They left from there and began a journey through Galilee, but he did not wish anyone to know about it. [31] He was teaching his disciples and telling them, "The Son of Man is to be handed over to men and they will kill him, and three days after his death he will rise." [32] But they did not understand the saying, and they were afraid to question him.
>
> [33] They came to Capernaum and, once inside the house, he began to ask them, "What were you arguing about on the way?" [34] But they remained silent. They had been discussing among themselves on the way who was the greatest. [35] Then he sat down, called the Twelve, and

said to them, "If anyone wishes to be first, he shall be the last of all and the servant of all." 36 Taking a child he placed it in their midst, and putting his arms around it he said to them, 37 "Whoever receives one child such as this in my name, receives me; and whoever receives me, receives not me but the One who sent me."

Lectio

Jesus and his disciples return through Galilee to their home village of Capernaum. The events at Caesarea Philippi and the Transfiguration are in the rear view and Jesus does his best to avoid areas where he might attract large crowds. On the way home Jesus issues his second "passion prediction." The first was delivered to shocked disciples in Caesarea Philippi. Now Jesus reminds them that the Son or Man (the self-referential title Jesus uses to reveal that he is the Messiah) will soon be handed over to men who will kill him. He continues to assure them that after three days in the tomb he will rise again. The disciples hear Jesus speak but do not understand this difficult saying, most notably the part about rising after being dead for three days. They are confident that they will be with him and so can protect him if needed. I think their silence here speaks volumes about their personal intent to protect Jesus from this point on.

Jesus and company enter the home of Andrew and Peter, which has been his ministry headquarters since his rejection in Nazareth two years earlier. In the privacy of that home, Jesus asks a direct question. "What were you arguing about on the way here?" There is no response. Jesus knows that some in the group had been arguing about who among them Jesus considered to be the greatest. Who was most favored by the Lord?

I believe that Jesus directs this question specifically to Peter, James, and John. These three had just shared the experience of the Transfiguration. On the slopes of Mount Hermon they had witnessed Jesus in his divine glory. They overheard his conversation with Moses and Elijah about the way that he would leave Jerusalem, his personal exodus event. Jesus had sworn them to secrecy. They were not to speak about this experience with anyone else until Jesus had risen from the grave. It is easy to imagine that each wonders who, among the three, is most favored by Jesus. Jesus cleverly answers his own question. He places a young child in their midst, teaching his gathered disciples that whoever receives a child like this, in his name, receives not only Jesus himself but also the Father who sent him.

Is there another hint given by the use of the child as a prop? That child would be the youngest male in the room, so Jesus may be using him to suggest that John, the youngest of the apostles, is most favored by Jesus. Tradition identifies John with the disciple "whom Jesus loved." He will sit in the most intimate position at the Last Supper (John 13:23). It will be to him that Jesus gives the care of his mother. John will be the only apostle to die of natural causes at the end of a long life of service to the Lord and the church. Read beyond the end of our Gospel selection this week and you will see that it is John who is emboldened to speak, and he does so without fear of reprisal. He says that he and his brother James had rebuked a man for driving out demons because he was not part of their group. Rather that castigating John (compare John 9:38–41 with what Jesus says to Peter in Mark 8:33, "Get behind me, Satan!"), Jesus gently corrects him as a teacher might correct a favorite student. This special relationship between Jesus and John will continue to grow as the Gospel narrative moves toward Jerusalem and the events of the passion. John will be with Jesus every step of the way.

Meditatio

Sometimes we hear what we want to hear and miss the message of the actual words. In this passage the apostles do not want to hear the passion predictions of Jesus. They want no part of a narrative anticipating arrest, suffering, death, burial, and then resurrection. Jesus explains clearly what awaits him in Jerusalem, but the apostles have "selective hearing" in reacting to this information. Their response is similar to our own when we hear news we don't want to process. They do not understand, but they fear that if they ask about it they will learn more than they can handle.

We can experience selective hearing too, especially when we come across the more difficult sayings of Jesus or struggle with things like the violence in the Old Testament. We don't understand and may be afraid to ask God. But questions are good and to be encouraged. The Hebrew Bible introduces us to characters who ask difficult questions. To characters who argue with God and engage God in protracted dialogue. Abraham questions God about how many righteous people God needs to find in Sodom to avoid destroying the city (Genesis 18:16–32). Moses challenges God with questions about God's stated intent to abandon his people after the golden calf incident and start over again with Moses (Exodus 32:9–14). Even Mary, the mother of Jesus, argues with Jesus about the need for more wine at the wedding in Cana (John 2:3–5). If you want to question God, go for it. You are in good company. Give it a try and see how your relationship with God grows this week.

Oratio

Psalm 116:12 (NLT) contains a wonderful question: "What can I offer the LORD for all he has done for me?" This question will be the core of our prayer this week. "What can I offer, Lord?" Show me the need and place me in a position to respond to that need with the same gentleness and compassion that you would offer in the same situation. Let my heart and my hands be yours in service this week.

Contemplatio

Who is greatest? That was the topic of the argument on the way home. Jesus says the greatest will be the last, the servant of all, and he will demonstrate what he means by this teaching at the Last Supper when he rises from the table, takes a bowl of water and a towel and surprises the gathered disciples again by washing their feet (see John 13:1–20). His greatness will be revealed in humble service to others—service that is unexpected and unsolicited. Jesus serves those who are not even aware that they need to be served.

We can participate in this same spiritual greatness when we open ourselves to opportunities to serve others in our family, in our church, in our local community, and in the larger world. Follow the example of Jesus this week and serve in some unexpected way.

OTHER READINGS: WISDOM 2:12, 17–20; JAMES 3:16—4:3

MILLSTONES AND STUMBLING BLOCKS

MARK 9:38–43, 45, 47–48

38 John said to him, "Teacher, we saw someone driving out demons in
your name, and we tried to prevent him because he does not follow us."
39 Jesus replied, "Do not prevent him. There is no one who performs
a mighty deed in my name who can at the same time speak ill of me.
40 For whoever is not against us is for us. 41 Anyone who gives you a cup
of water to drink because you belong to Christ, amen, I say to you, will
surely not lose his reward.

42 "Whoever causes one of these little ones who believe [in me] to sin, it
would be better for him if a great millstone were put around his neck
and he were thrown into the sea. 43 If your hand causes you to sin, cut
it off. It is better for you to enter into life maimed than with two hands
to go into Gehenna, into the unquenchable fire.

45 "And if your foot causes you to sin, cut it off. It is better for you to
enter into life crippled than with two feet to be thrown into Gehenna.

47 "And if your eye causes you to sin, pluck it out. Better for you to enter into
the kingdom of God with one eye than with two eyes to be thrown into
Gehenna, 48 where 'their worm does not die, and the fire is not quenched.'"

Lectio

In this Gospel reading the youngest apostle (John, the brother of James) has the loudest voice. Jesus called these two the "Sons of Thunder" (Mark 3:17) and here John seems to be motivated by a holy zeal to stop others who are doing good without the disciples' authorization. John tells Jesus that he came across a man casting out demons in the name of Jesus—but he is "not one of us" and John thinks he should be silenced. Exorcists of this sort were common in antiquity. Recall that in the book of Acts the seven sons of a Jewish priest named Sceva get a rude surprise when they try to cast our demons in the name of "Jesus whom Paul preaches" (Acts 19:11–20).

Jesus will have none of this. As their leader he is certainly aware of the demands on loyalty needed to keep a group of Middle Eastern men together. But Jesus wants to expand the boundaries of these bonds of loyalty and include those working toward the same goals—in this case to free a person from the oppression of the devil. Good work done in service of others should not be stopped. This volunteer is on their side and will not be inclined to speak against Jesus and his ministry.

The scene shifts. Now Jesus is with the disciples in a private setting. He addresses the apostles and warns them that they are responsible for the "little ones who believe" in him. "Little ones" is not a reference to children but rather to grown men and women who have responded to the preaching of Jesus and are just beginning to grow in faith. In Mark 10:24, Jesus refers to the apostolic group as his "children" when he teaches them how hard it will be for those caught up in the entanglements of wealth to enter the kingdom of God. Here Jesus wants the disciples to know that the way they live as his followers will be an example for newcomers to follow. They need to take to heart the seriousness of being a good witness and avoiding any activity that would lead someone into sin.

The punishment threatened for misleading the "little ones" is called worse than being drowned in the Sea of Galilee by a millstone. Punishment by drowning was known during this period, and abhorrent to Jews. A millstone—a donut-shaped stone used to grind grain—eventually wears out, and many were repurposed as boat anchors. This graphic image would not be lost on the apostles, many of whom were commercial fishermen. Jesus is giving them a serious warning.

The teaching that follows helps us appreciate the difference between the literal and the literary meaning of a biblical text. Does Jesus literally mean us to cut off a hand if it causes us to sin? Or to pluck out an eye that is leading us to sinful activity? The answer is an emphatic no! The literary style of this teaching—hyperbole—reveals the seriousness of any activity that a follower of Jesus engages in that might drive people away from faith. Eternal destinies are in the balance. Better to err on the side of caution and pastoral concern for others than face the fires of hell. The choice is ours. The better choice is clear.

Meditatio

What is a "stumbling block" (verse 42, NRSV), and how could the disciples place one before a new follower, a "little one" in Jesus's company? Other English translations reveal that a "stumbling block" is anything that causes these little ones to sin. The Bible defines sin as a condition of alienation and separation from God. The Bible teaches that sinful activity typically starts small and then works to distort our judgment. One might wonder why any sinful activity is harmful in the long run, or why a loving God would not give us a pass for small transgressions. The problem is that sin grows. Left unchecked (not acknowledged and repented from) it always gets bigger and will lead to spiritual death. Patterns of habitual sin can even cascade down through generations and affect our children and grandchildren; they are more likely to follow a sinful example set before them. The echoes of our sinful actions can last long beyond our own lives. That is why Jesus is so adamant in his teaching about the subject.

How do we place a "stumbling block" in the way of a believer? When we are not aware that our actions speak louder than our words. The witness of the works of our hands, the places our feet take us, the things that our eyes take in (and thus what our minds dwell on)—all these speak to others about the way we love and follow the Lord. Our hands need to stop doing anything that would bring shame to Jesus. Our feet must not take us down paths that lead to destruction. We must do our best, with the help of God's grace, to be faith-filled stewards of our eyes since they are the window to our soul. People—"little ones" who are just beginning their journey of faith—are watching us and will follow our example. Jesus uses us to reveal who he is to the world. Let's take this commission seriously this week.

Oratio

Lord Jesus, my hands, my feet, and my eyes are each a gift from the Father. Give me the grace to use them in your service so that I can be a light that shines in the darkness, a lamp set on a stand that gives light to all in the room. Amen.

Contemplatio

This week be especially aware of how outward actions reveal the inner life of faith that we have in the Lord. As I have written before and want to remind you once again: in many circumstances you may be the only Bible the people you encounter will ever read. We learn in the letter to the Hebrews that the written Word of God is living and active (Hebrews 4:12). It should be just as alive and active in the way that we live in the world. The way that we live our faith, the way that we express our faith, and how that faith is "read" by others is our unique call as followers of Jesus.

We are also challenged this week to keep our eyes on the prize and not on the allure of our popular culture or the news media, to resist the siren call of the world and its many bedazzlements. Pray for the grace you will need to keep your eyes, your hands, your feet, and your heart only on Jesus. This will not be easy and will require diligence on your part, but the effort becomes its own reward.

OTHER READINGS: NUMBERS 11:25–29; JAMES 5:1–6

TWENTY-SEVENTH SUNDAY IN ORDINARY TIME

HARDENED HEARTS

MARK 10:2–10

2 The Pharisees approached and asked, "Is it lawful for a husband to
divorce his wife?" They were testing him. 3 He said to them in reply,
"What did Moses command you?" 4 They replied, "Moses permitted
him to write a bill of divorce and dismiss her." 5 But Jesus told them,
"Because of the hardness of your hearts he wrote you this commandment. 6 But from the beginning of creation, 'God made them male
and female. 7 For this reason a man shall leave his father and mother
[and be joined to his wife], 8 and the two shall become one flesh.' So
they are no longer two but one flesh. 9 Therefore what God has joined
together, no human being must separate." 10 In the house the disciples
again questioned him about this.

The Gospel opens with a question posed by Pharisees who challenge Jesus to a public debate. What does Jesus teach about the possibility of divorce? In the Middle East an open question like this is a challenge to your honor. This one is a classic "gotcha," intended to shame Jesus by forcing him into a bad choice. Like any teacher questioned publicly in this way, Jesus turns the tables by responding to their question with one of his own. It is a familiar tactic of his, seen in many similar passages that show Jesus as a master of the question-and-response honor-and-shame encounter.

"Is it lawful for a man to divorce his wife?" Jesus's response—"What did Moses command you?"—puts the Pharisees on the defensive. They must first reveal their own position in their reply that Moses "permitted" a man to write a certificate of dismissal (which would have to be reviewed by a council of elders before he could divorce his wife; see Deuteronomy 24:1–4). Jesus has them on the ropes! He tells the Pharisees that Moses agreed to this practice as a concession to hard hearts. Then he reminds them that it was not that way in the beginning. God's perfect plan for marriage is laid out in the first two chapters of Genesis (he quotes from Genesis 1:27 and 2:24). Jesus concludes that "therefore"—logically, obviously—what God joins, no human being should separate.

The problem is with human beings. We are prone to a "hardness of heart" toward God's plans. We want to do things our own way. God allowed for divorce in the law of Moses as a concession to our sinful nature.

Later, in the house and away from the crowds, his disciples have a question for Jesus about this teaching (Mark 10:10–12). Notice that away from the public forum the disciples can ask a direct question and get a direct answer. Their questions are not perceived as a challenge by Jesus. They want to understand the fullness of his teaching about marriage and divorce. Jesus is clear. Anyone who divorces his wife in order to marry another person commits adultery against her.

Marriages in biblical times are arranged between families. Divorce is serious and costly. It strains the bond of both the married couple and the extended family on both sides. Jesus holds the standard for marriage very high and his disciples will have to do so as well.

Meditatio

Marriage is hard work. Any married person appreciates what it takes to keep a marriage bond active, growing, and intact. In the culture of our Western world we typically meet a potential mate, grow in love, and hope that our families will agree with our choice of marriage partner. In the Middle Eastern world of Jesus, potential mates meet after careful arrangements. The respective parents present their children to each other as perfectly suited for marriage and then trust that the two will become one through the marriage bond and the active support of extended family and the faith community. Sadly, this sort of engaged support is not always present in our marriages today. This can put a couple at a disadvantage from the outset and will strain the marriage bond.

Jesus said that he would be with us always, even to the end of the age, and that where two or three are gathered together in his name he will be in their midst. In a Christian marriage two people become one. Jesus is present in that union. Dissolving that bond for any reason is serious business and should not be considered lightly. The disciples understand this. In the parallel passage in Matthew's Gospel, they respond to Jesus by saying, "If that is the case of a man with his wife, it is better not to marry" (Matthew 19:10). Jesus sets the bar high and wants those who follow him to do their best to reach for that height in their married lives.

Oratio

Two verses provide prayerful insight for marriage this week. Pray with them for your own marriage, for the marriage of your parents, your siblings, your friends, and even for your co-workers.

"Be strong and courageous. Do not be afraid; do not be discouraged, for the LORD your God will be with you wherever you go." (Joshua 1:9 NIV)

"It is my prayer that your love may abound more and more, with knowledge and all discernment, so that you may approve what is excellent, and so be pure and blameless for the day of Christ." (Philippians 1:9–10 ESV)

Contemplatio

"Because of the hardness of your hearts …" What does Jesus mean when he uses these words to explain why Moses wrote the commandment that allows for divorce (under strict conditions) in Deuteronomy 24? This phrase will remind the disciples of the book of Exodus and the promise God makes to Moses that the heart of Pharaoh will be "hardened" so he will initially be unable to respond to the plagues that are intended to change his heart (that is, his mind) and let God's people leave Egypt (Exodus 4:21, 7:3). This "hardening" does not so much refer to God placing an impenetrable shell around the heart as to God's repeated attempts to squeeze Pharaoh's heart to see what is inside (like making a sponge hard). Is there anything within that might allow Pharaoh to respond to God's messenger, Moses? Re-read the plague narratives this week (they begin in Exodus 7). They work! Slowly but surely God gets Pharaoh's undivided attention and Pharaoh commands Moses and the Israelites to leave Egypt so that they can move on to the Promised Land.

Has your heart ever been hard? Do you recall times when God may have been "squeezing" you to see if there was something in you that could respond to a call? To a mission? To a particular need in the church? Use this week to be aware of the ways that God is getting your attention so that you can be ready to respond to God's call in your life.

OTHER READINGS: GENESIS 2:18–24; HEBREWS 2:9–11

TWENTY-EIGHTH SUNDAY IN ORDINARY TIME

WHERE IS YOUR SECURITY?

MARK 10:17–30

[17] As he was setting out on a journey, a man ran up, knelt down before
him, and asked him, "Good teacher, what must I do to inherit eternal
life?" [18] Jesus answered him, "Why do you call me good? No one is
good but God alone. [19] You know the commandments: 'You shall not
kill; you shall not commit adultery; you shall not steal; you shall not
bear false witness; you shall not defraud; honor your father and your
mother.'" [20] He replied and said to him, "Teacher, all of these I have

observed from my youth.” 21 Jesus, looking at him, loved him and said
to him, “You are lacking in one thing. Go, sell what you have, and give
to [the] poor and you will have treasure in heaven; then come, follow
me.” 22 At that statement his face fell, and he went away sad, for he had
many possessions.

23 Jesus looked around and said to his disciples, “How hard it is for those
who have wealth to enter the kingdom of God!” 24 The disciples were
amazed at his words. So Jesus again said to them in reply, “Children,
how hard it is to enter the kingdom of God! 25 It is easier for a camel to
pass through [the] eye of [a] needle than for one who is rich to enter the
kingdom of God.” 26 They were exceedingly astonished and said among
themselves, “Then who can be saved?” 27 Jesus looked at them and
said, “For human beings it is impossible, but not for God. All things
are possible for God.” 28 Peter began to say to him, “We have given up
everything and followed you.” 29 Jesus said, “Amen, I say to you, there
is no one who has given up house or brothers or sisters or mother or
father or children or lands for my sake and for the sake of the gospel
30 who will not receive a hundred times more now in this present age:
houses and brothers and sisters and mothers and children and lands,
with persecutions, and eternal life in the age to come.”

Lectio

Why does Jesus always respond to a public question with a question of his own? In this week’s Gospel a rich man runs up to Jesus in the street and falls at his feet in an obvious effort to interrupt his journey. He greets Jesus in this very public setting by addressing him as “Good teacher.” Then he asks what he needs to do to inherit eternal life.

Does he think he has put Jesus on the spot? To discern what is driving this man, Jesus responds with a question of his own. He wants to know why the man refers to him as “good.” Surely he knows that God alone is good? Is the man attempting to shame Jesus with a false compliment? Or is this a heartfelt request for information about eternal life? Jesus concludes it is the latter and answers the question. (We learn in Matthew 19:20 that the man is still young.)

Jesus reminds the man about the commandments of the law that deal with our duty to others—the horizontally themed commandments that make for solid interpersonal relationships in a community of believers. These commandments are rooted in honor of father and mother. If you get that one right you will not be likely to commit adultery or murder, bring false witness, or steal from another. The young man assures Jesus that he has kept all these commands since his youth—and the implication is that he still feels distant from God.

Jesus is impressed. He looks at the man with love. For Jesus feels this young man is close to becoming a disciple. In the New Testament the word *love* includes the idea of attachment. Jesus feels an attachment for the young man and invites him into the discipleship group—if he can do just one more thing: sell all that he has and give it to the poor. Jesus challenges him to divest himself of his identity, his security. His possessions—his family of origin, his boyhood home, and the land that supports both—cannot easily be liquidated. Jesus asks the man to leave them behind. If he can trust Jesus in this, he can follow. It is a tall order and one that, at least initially, the young man is unwilling to follow. He has many possessions.

The other disciples are put off by what they have witnessed. Jesus reminds them how hard it will be for anyone who trusts in riches (the security of family, home, land) to enter the kingdom of God. They wonder who then can be saved. They have always thought of wealth as a blessing from God, not something that would keep you from responding to God's call. Jesus does not back down. Instead, he presents an image of impossibility: that of a camel trying to fit through the eye of a needle! But there might be a way. Jesus tells the apostles that this is impossible for humans—but not for God; for God all things are possible.

Peter suddenly gets it. He recalls that three years earlier he was in the same position as that young man. Peter was well off, living with his wife in a nice home in the village. He captained a fishing vessel and worked with his father and other local associates. He was set for life—and then he was surprised by grace and found himself responding to the same challenge of Jesus: Leave your nets behind and follow me. Peter and the other apostles have all left behind the security of family, home, and livelihood to follow

Jesus. Once it would have seemed impossible for Peter to consider such a call, but now here he is—because nothing is impossible with God.

Meditatio

What have camels and needles to do with each other? What message is Jesus trying to convey with this odd juxtaposition of images? Anyone considering this "wisdom" saying will conclude that there is no chance of a camel passing through the eye of a needle. Jesus confirms his intention when he tells the disciples that humanly it is impossible for a rich man to leave family, house, and land—but for God all things are possible. Forget anything you may have heard about a "camel pass" in the mountains or an "eye of the needle gate" allowing camels access to an ancient city. Both explanations are just clever attempts to get around a hard teaching. Jesus is concerned about our attitude toward our possessions.

Our wealth comes to us as a gift from God and we should be willing to return it to God when needs arise. We cannot be greedy with our possessions and hope to please the Lord. We are rich with heaven's treasures when we are willing to put our gifts and talents at God's disposal, so they can be used to support the church, serve the poor, and reveal the kingdom of God breaking forth in the world. Our generosity will be a sign of God working within us. Jesus is calling us away from "possessing" our gifts, talents, and abilities and encouraging us to share them with others. It may at times seem impossible; rather like trying to fit an ornery camel through the eye of a needle. But what is impossible for man is possible for God.

Oratio

I love this prayer of abandonment to God's loving plan for our life: *Lord, teach me not only to accept, but to truly love my littleness and my inner poverty, and to place my trust in your infinite goodness and mercy, that I might be entirely dependent upon your protective, fatherly care and experience the transforming power of your grace in my life this week. Amen.*

Contemplatio

Jesus challenges a rich man to sell everything and give to the poor the security that his wealth provided. If he could do this he could return to

Jesus and join the growing group of disciples. The question we should ask ourselves this week is simple. What are we willing to leave behind—what do we *need* to leave behind—to accept Jesus's invitation to follow him?

St. Francis took these words of Jesus literally and left his family, his home, and his estate to turn toward God and a life of faith. He even left behind the clothes provided by his wealthy father and spent the rest of his life in service of Italy's poor. If Jesus challenged you to sell all you have and give it to the poor, what would be the first thing you put on Craigslist?

Think about your life and what you value. Where is your security? Is it in your family? Things you own? Your capabilities? Your investments? How would you respond to this challenge of Jesus if he looked at you with love and promised that if you could leave these things behind you could become his disciple and enter a new family of faith where you will receive back new houses, brothers, sisters, fathers, children, and fields? Would you take the risk? What would you have to lose?

Consider how this sort of reversal—where the poor are elevated and the rich come down a peg or two—is something the poor readily respond to. It is not as appealing to those of us who are rich. The rich have much to lose and may leave Jesus grieving. But Peter and the other apostles have already passed this test. They recall how they were able to walk away from the security of their earlier lives to say yes to Jesus. And they are experiencing the blessings he promised—and persecutions too. Say yes to Jesus this week and you will find yourself in some very fine company indeed! What seems impossible for man is possible for God.

OTHER READINGS: WISDOM 7:7–11; HEBREWS 4:12–13

TWENTY-NINTH SUNDAY IN ORDINARY TIME

WHAT DO YOU WANT ME TO DO FOR YOU?

MARK 10:35–45

> [35] Then James and John, the sons of Zebedee, came to him and said to
> him, "Teacher, we want you to do for us whatever we ask of you." [36] He

> replied, “What do you wish [me] to do for you?” 37 They answered him, “Grant that in your glory we may sit one at your right and the other at your left.” 38 Jesus said to them, “You do not know what you are asking. Can you drink the cup that I drink or be baptized with the baptism with which I am baptized?” 39 They said to him, “We can.” Jesus said to them, “The cup that I drink, you will drink, and with the baptism with which I am baptized, you will be baptized; 40 but to sit at my right or at my left is not mine to give but is for those for whom it has been prepared.” 41 When the ten heard this, they became indignant at James and John. 42 Jesus summoned them and said to them, “You know that those who are recognized as rulers over the Gentiles lord it over them, and their great ones make their authority over them felt. 43 But it shall not be so among you. Rather, whoever wishes to be great among you will be your servant; 44 whoever wishes to be first among you will be the slave of all. 45 For the Son of Man did not come to be served but to serve and to give his life as a ransom for many.”

Lectio

This is the second time in this Gospel that we meet James and John. We encountered them earlier when Jesus calls them into the apostolic group (Mark 3:17) and names them “sons of thunder”—a probable reference to the booming voice of their father Zebedee, who worked alongside his sons to fish the waters of the Sea of Galilee. When Jesus likes someone, he gives them a special name, as Simon is called Peter, referring to the rock-like character of the man who would come to lead the Twelve.

Now Zebedee’s two sons approach Jesus with a bold request. They want a favor. Jesus plays along and responds to their opening ploy with a question of his own, effectively turning the tables on the upstarts. “What do you wish me to do for you [two]?” James and John respond that they want to be seated on the right and left side of Jesus when he takes his throne. Recall that they were present when Jesus was transfigured before them and was revealed to these two—and Peter—in his divine glory. Now James and John are acting as a team to secure the best seats in the house when Jesus takes care of business in Jerusalem.

Jesus responds patiently. He tells them that they do not know what they ask. He has just barely finished telling them that he is going to Jerusalem to lay down his life (Mark 10:32–34). James and John are not able to hear and understand this part of the prediction of Jesus's passion and death.

Jesus wonders aloud if James and John believe they are able to drink the cup that Jesus will be called to drink. This is a cultural reference and reveals the role of a Middle Eastern father/patriarch, who pours a cup of wine for everyone assembled at his table. Guests are expected to drink it—all of it—to honor the host. Jesus may also be referencing the "cup of acceptance," the fourth cup of the Passover ritual, which is consumed at the end of the celebration with a prayer that those drinking the cup can accept what God has in store for them in the coming year. In either case Jesus indicates that he cannot grant their request. Those seats have been reserved by the Father and will go to those for whom they are assigned.

Now the other ten apostles chime in. They are indignant with the brothers. More to the point, they are angry they did not think of this ploy themselves! In the Middle East it is every man, or every set of brothers, for themselves. Each apostle has a unique relationship with Jesus, but not necessarily with the others. Jockeying for a more honorable position at the table is culturally expected. James and John saw their chance and took it. The others felt left out and understandably express their displeasure.

Jesus uses their indignant response to his advantage. He compares the leadership style of their Roman overlords who keep the peace with a boot on your neck with the leadership that will be required of the apostles. They will not be allowed to "lord it over" anyone. To be the greatest they will have to become the servant of all. Jesus, as the Son of Man—the Messiah—says that he came to serve, not to be served. He came to give his life away as a ransom for many. They will learn more about this kind of leadership when they finally arrive in Jerusalem in only a few weeks' time.

Meditatio

Jesus asks James and John, "What is it you want me to do for you?" (NRSV). Imagine that Jesus appeared to you and asked you the same question. What would your response be? I doubt that you would be so bold as to make a request similar to that of the "sons of thunder." I still wonder how I would respond. Perhaps my request would be for a healing needed by someone that I love. Maybe it would be for a greater bounty in my work-aday efforts to secure a living for my family. Could I find the boldness to ask for world peace? The end of physical pain associated with famine and drought? That the Fighting Irish of Notre Dame would win just one more national championship in my lifetime? (Just kidding with that one.) Take a few moments this week to consider how you might answer Jesus if he directed this question to you. "What is it you want me to do for you?"

Oratio

American theologian Reinhold Niebuhr wrote the Serenity Prayer as a way to seek the grace of God that we need to live a life that will honor God in all that we say and do: *God, grant me the serenity to accept the things that I cannot change, courage to change the things I can, and wisdom to know the difference.*

Contemplatio

What does servant leadership mean to you? Jesus will demonstrate his type of leadership in the middle of the Last Supper when he wraps a towel around his waist and begins to wash each of the apostles' feet. When Jesus completes this act of service he commands them that "you also should do as I have done for you." (John 13:15 NRSV). Can you imagine a servant leadership opportunity in your church community? In your neighborhood? At your next family gathering? In your marriage or among your siblings? Be open to this call and remember that Jesus reminds us in this Gospel that he, the Son of Man, did not come from the Father to be served but rather to serve—even if that meant he would have to lay down his life as a ransom for many. Our expressions of servant leadership may not be as bold as those of Jesus, but we can still follow his example in laying down our lives, our schedules, our free time—even our cell phones?—for the sake of others as we work tirelessly to see the Kingdom of God break forth in our world.

OTHER READINGS: ISAIAH 53:10–11; HEBREWS 4:14–16

HE KEPT CALLING

MARK 10:46–52

46 They came to Jericho. And as he was leaving Jericho with his disciples
and a sizable crowd, Bartimaeus, a blind man, the son of Timaeus, sat
by the roadside begging. 47 On hearing that it was Jesus of Nazareth, he
began to cry out and say, "Jesus, son of David, have pity on me." 48 And
many rebuked him, telling him to be silent. But he kept calling out all
the more, "Son of David, have pity on me." 49 Jesus stopped and said,
"Call him." So they called the blind man, saying to him, "Take courage;
get up, he is calling you." 50 He threw aside his cloak, sprang up, and
came to Jesus. 51 Jesus said to him in reply, "What do you want me
to do for you?" The blind man replied to him, "Master, I want to see."
52 Jesus told him, "Go your way; your faith has saved you." Immediately
he received his sight and followed him on the way.

Lectio

Jesus and the ever-growing band of disciples have made their way to Jericho and apparently intend to pass through without pausing to refresh themselves before starting the steep ascent toward Jerusalem. Jericho was a city rich in history and tradition, known for offering hospitality to all who entered her gates. The Bible credits the prophet Elisha with a miraculous intervention that made the salt-laden local water sweet (2 Kings 2:15–22). The area surrounding the city produced some of the best fruit in the region. Pilgrims anticipated coming to the city and sampling its delights. Jesus seems intent on simply passing through without stopping. To reach his friends in Bethany by nightfall he has to keep on the move.

Jesus is surrounded by a large crowd. Middle Eastern leaders move slowly, for they are typically surrounded by supporters who act as "human shields" and can close ranks in case of assault. Knowing this, we can imagine that some of the disciples in the front of the group will meet Bartimaeus before Jesus passes by. Most English translation of the Gospel label

Bartimaeus as a blind beggar, which is somewhat misleading. "Begging" does not accurately reflect what Bartimaeus is doing by the roadside.

In Jewish religious practice the faithful are bound by the law to pray, to fast, and to give alms. Daily prayer is both public and private. Fasting is a single-day requirement on the feast of Yom Kippur. Almsgiving is to be practiced at every available opportunity. To give alms to a worthy person is a "mitzvah," a good deed that leads to a blessing from God. The rabbinic sages in the time of Jesus had reasoned that if religious Jews are required to give alms, God would be required to provide them with almsworthy recipients. This is the role Bartimaeus fills in Jericho. He is stationed at the gate a traveler has to pass through to take the road to the holy city of Jerusalem. If you are going that way, more than likely you are going to offer a sacrifice or make a donation to the temple. You would welcome the opportunity to give alms to those in need along the way.

Now we meet Bartimaeus. He has the heightened sense of sound common to the blind. He can hear the chatter of the crowd surrounding Jesus. Were they speaking of the amazing works Jesus has done? Likely so. Bartimaeus knows it is time to act. He has to stop this Jesus so that the good people who accompany him will have an opportunity to share their alms with him. But how to stop the progress of such a large crowd?

Bartimaeus draws on his booming voice. He cries to Jesus as the Son of David to have mercy on him. Warned sternly to be silent, he knows he is gaining the attention of the crowd so he cries out even louder: "Son of David, have pity on me." The title "Son of David" is clearly Messianic. Jesus hears him and plays along. Notice that Jesus tells someone to "call him here" (NRSV)—sort of a royal summons by the gate. Next, Jesus plays the part of a city elder: "What do you want me to do for you?" It might seem obvious to us that he wants his sight restored, but remember that in his current condition he can collect alms from pilgrims to support his family. We should be somewhat surprised to hear that he wants to see! Jesus acts. His eyes are opened and now he has little choice but to follow Jesus. His days as an almsworthy recipient are ended. Now he heralds Jesus's ability to heal. The blind can see! He will gladly follow Jesus and tell his story to all who will listen.

Meditatio

What do you think motivated the disciples near Jesus to rebuke a blind man crying out for mercy? Was their concern for Jesus? For themselves? Perhaps they concluded that Jesus should not be delayed by a nobody. Maybe they had a schedule to keep with fifteen miles of difficult climbing between them and Bethany? They seem convinced that Jesus should not be bothered by a person like Bartimaeus. My goodness, were they wrong.

Are you intrigued by the blind man and his persistence? I am. His efforts paid off in a big way. If we follow his example it seems to indicate that we can pester God a bit in calling for an act of mercy. Jesus taught his disciples to ask, to seek, and to knock (Matthew 7:7–8) until the question is answered, the lost item is found, and the door is finally opened. Persistence is the point of this teaching. Persistence in prayer. Who asks only once, or looks for a lost item in a single place, or knocks on the door with only a single rap of a knuckle? Bartimaeus is our example of persistence this week. He knows who Jesus is (the healing prophet from Nazareth) and does his best to gain his attention and secure healing. His eyes are opened, the darkness of his blindness vanquished, and he responds immediately by following Jesus on the road that leads to the Mount of Olives—and the triumphant entrance into Jerusalem the following day.

Oratio

Dear Lord, you opened the eyes of the blind so they could see. Restore my spiritual sight this week so that I can see again, and like Bartimaeus follow you, speaking boldly about your love and mercy that I have experienced in my life. Amen

Contemplatio

Giving alms. It is a requirement in the Jewish faith. You trust that if God wants us to give alms, then God will present us with almsworthy persons. How can we participate in this "mitzvah" of almsgiving in our daily lives? How are we to know if the person God puts in front of us is deserving or not? This calls for maturity and discernment. Personally, I lean into our local bishop's charity outreach project. Each year I commit a portion of my income to the bishop, who directs those in his employ to distribute funds to the almsworthy persons in our community. I know some of the people who work with the Bishop in this outreach and they assure me that my contributions do reach the most vulnerable and needy around us. I don't stop there. I also pray for the bishop and his service team before I make my contribution. I pray that the Holy Spirit will guide those who know about the immediate needs to make the right decisions as they go forth and give alms in the name of Jesus. Maybe this is a way that you too can participate in the almsgiving "mitzvah" this week.

OTHER READINGS: JEREMIAH 31:7–9; HEBREWS 5:1–6

ALL SAINTS

BEATITUDE CHALLENGES

MATTHEW 5:1–12a

1 When he saw the crowds, he went up the mountain, and after he had
sat down, his disciples came to him. 2 He began to teach them, saying:

3 "Blessed are the poor in spirit,
for theirs is the kingdom of heaven.
4 Blessed are they who mourn,
for they will be comforted.
5 Blessed are the meek,
for they will inherit the land.
6 Blessed are they who hunger and thirst for righteousness,
for they will be satisfied.
7 Blessed are the merciful,
for they will be shown mercy.
8 Blessed are the clean of heart,
for they will see God.
9 Blessed are the peacemakers,
for they will be called children of God.

[10] Blessed are they who are persecuted for the sake of righteousness,
for theirs is the kingdom of heaven.

[11] Blessed are you when they insult you and persecute you and utter
every kind of evil against you [falsely] because of me. [12] Rejoice and
be glad, for your reward will be great in heaven."

Lectio

In our Gospel, Jesus opens his Sermon on the Mount with the beatitudes. What are we to make of these challenging statements about the Kingdom of God? What is the intent of our Lord as he engages his disciples at the base of a mountain? We can start to answer these and other challenging questions by looking to the summary of Jesus's early ministry that Matthew provides just before our passage begins.

At the end of Matthew's fourth chapter we learn that from a base in Capernaum Jesus has moved around Galilee, "teaching in their synagogues, proclaiming the gospel of the kingdom, and curing every disease and illness among the people.... And great crowds from Galilee, the Decapolis, Jerusalem, and Judea, and from beyond the Jordan followed him" (Matthew 4:23–25). Jesus followed a precise plan. His was a threefold ministry of healing, preaching, and then teaching—and in that specific order! This is an important insight into Jesus and his initial success in Galilee.

Jesus was a wonder-working healer who drew great crowds in response to the healing miracles that people experienced and witnessed daily. The swelling crowds would be engaged by Jesus's preaching—"proclaiming the gospel of the kingdom." Inspired by the preaching, potential students—disciples—came to be taught by this fascinating Rabbi. Watch for this order as we experience Jesus as preacher in the beatitudes, a series of "gospel of the kingdom" statements used to inspire and connect current and potential disciples to himself and his movement. Each one is intended as a spark that might ignite curiosity among some in the crowd.

The site of the Sermon on the Mount has been reliably identified as a natural amphitheater just west of the city of Capernaum. Thousands have now arrived, drawn away from the commerce of the city center in the mid-morning hours when, after a full night of commercial fishing and sorting the catch for market, the locals have a few hours of free time before they need to rest.

Jesus is aware of the ebb and flow of Capernaum's working-class people. Now he moves with them to the amphitheater where he takes a seat, the position of honor accorded a teacher in the Middle East. The teacher sits and the students stand to listen. When he speaks from the base of the hill his voice would carry up the slopes to the teeming crowds. Jesus begins with a series of pithy statements that push his listeners toward a decision. Are you in or out? With us or not?

Each beatitude opens with "blessed." The word is hard to translate; it includes a flavor of "happy" and "well off." Another helpful translation is "honored," meaning that God will honor those who take on one or more of these Kingdom values in their lives. God will honor the poor in spirit, those who mourn, and the meek. The list goes on.

We learn that God will even honor those who are persecuted and that potential disciples will be honored even when they are insulted. Jesus promises that they will rejoice and be glad when they are persecuted, just as the prophets were of old. What does he mean? In Matthew 23:37 Jesus laments that the nation, symbolized by its capital city and its leaders, kills the prophets and those sent to proclaim a message of God's kingdom. The same fate might befall those who become disciples of Jesus.

The beatitudes reveal the genius of Jesus as preacher. Each is intended to spark a response. Those willing to be "poor in spirit" will be rewarded for their dependence on God. Any potential disciple willing to mourn rather than seek revenge will be welcome in his company.

Jesus is looking for disciples who are merciful and clean of heart. What does it mean to be "clean in heart"? The Middle East views all thought processes as emotively infused. You think with your heart. To be "pure in heart" means that potential disciples have their mind focused on the things of God. If your heart is so cleansed, then you will be able to be a peacemaker rather than a peace-breaker. As a disciple you will be required to suffer persecution rather than actively resist.

Who is up to the challenge? A wildly successful healing ministry has drawn a huge crowd. Jesus preaches the beatitudes to inspire and connect some to his vision. He will follow up on this preaching when he reveals himself as Israel's new and authentic teacher in the rest of the Sermon on the Mount. Healing, preaching, and then teaching. It worked for Jesus then, and it will work in our ministries now.

In our meditation this week I want you to focus on a single challenging beatitude: "Blessed are the meek, for they will inherit the land." If God honors the meek and gives them the land, won't bullies come and take it back by force? How will anyone who is meek be able to withstand such an assault? I struggled with this beatitude before I discovered a key to understanding what Jesus is teaching. The key is defining "meek" in its biblical context. Look at Numbers 12:3. This passage presents Moses as very meek, more so than anyone else on earth. Some translations translate the word as "humble"; the words are synonymous. What is going on here? How can we honor Moses for being the most humble/meek man on earth? It seems like hyperbole until you understand that the Bible's use of the word conveys a sense and expectation of having one's strength under control, of full dependence on God. It is used to describe Moses in Numbers 12:3 because he does not defend himself when his leadership and authority are challenged by his elder siblings. He keeps his great strength under God's control and waits for God to intervene. And God does. It's a great story—give it a read.

When Jesus honors the meek who will inherit the land he means that God will honor any would-be disciples willing to put their strength under God's control. They will be uniquely suited to receive and hold on to the gift of the land. These are the kind of leaders that Jesus is looking for. What is your particular strength? What is your gift, talent, or ability? Have you placed that under God's control so that it can be used in the world for God's glory and honor? That is the challenge of this particular beatitude.

There are seven more! Later, read each beatitude with the idea of a challenge in mind and then ask yourself which one, among the eight, resonates most deeply with you.

Oratio

You really can't teach the beatitudes. They can only be preached. Jesus intends to inspire potential disciples into action. He is trying to stir our souls into a real-world response. Join me. Take the step. Here we go. Our prayer this week will inspire us as well.

"Come Holy Spirit and fill the hearts of your faithful and enkindle in them the fire of your love. Send forth your Spirit and they shall be created, and through them you will renew the face of the earth."

Contemplatio

Can we put our faith into action this week? Which of the beatitude challenges of Jesus inspire you to Christian service and outreach? Take a few moments and prayerfully review each of the "action" challenges that can be sourced from the beatitudes. Can you lean into the Lord this week, acknowledging that you are "poor in Spirit" and therefore need to rely on the Lord in a new way? What would it look like to hunger and thirst for living in a way that will please God? Where can we find an opportunity to show someone mercy? To help someone simply because we have the ability and wherewithal to do so? Can you be a peacemaker in your community, in your family? What would that look like this week? The possible applications of the beatitudes are plentiful. Choose one and lean in!

OTHER READINGS: REVELATION 7:2–4, 9–14; 1 JOHN 3:1–3

THIRTY-FIRST SUNDAY IN ORDINARY TIME

STARTING POINT

MARK 12:28–34

28 One of the scribes, when he came forward and heard them disputing
and saw how well he had answered them, asked him, "Which is the first
of all the commandments?" 29 Jesus replied, "The first is this: 'Hear, O
Israel! The Lord our God is Lord alone! 30 You shall love the Lord your
God with all your heart, with all your soul, with all your mind, and with

all your strength.' [31] The second is this: 'You shall love your neighbor as yourself.' There is no other commandment greater than these." [32] The scribe said to him, "Well said, teacher. You are right in saying, 'He is One and there is no other than he.' [33] And 'to love him with all your heart, with all your understanding, with all your strength, and to love your neighbor as yourself' is worth more than all burnt offerings and sacrifices." [34] And when Jesus saw that [he] answered with understanding, he said to him, "You are not far from the kingdom of God." And no one dared to ask him any more questions.

Lectio

Jesus is on the temple mount in the ancient city of Jerusalem. He has just confounded the Sadducees and left them speechless. A scribe comes on the scene and is impressed by how Jesus has put these temple-based religious authorities in their place. The scribe asks Jesus a direct question in a very public setting and to our surprise Jesus answers him without delay. Up to this point in Mark's Gospel, whenever someone asks Jesus a public question he has responded with a question of his own. This technique is often employed in the Middle East to determine if the questioner is friend or foe. But not this time. There appears to be a level of trust between Jesus and the scribe, for the question can have no wrong answer and actually offers any teacher a platform from which to expound. "Which commandment is the first of all?" (NRSV). There are 613 commandments to choose from. Jesus's answer will set the stage for a deeper conversation to follow.

A scribe at this time was a religious official required to have an extensive knowledge of the Bible. They were honored as the learned guardians of the Law of God. Scribes could also draft legal documents, marriage and divorce contracts, loans, and bills of sale for land. Every village in Israel had at least one resident scribe. Jesus honors the office when he states that "every scribe who has been trained for the kingdom of heaven is like the master of a household who brings out of his treasure what is new and what is old" (Matthew 13:51–52).

This scribe impresses Jesus. Jesus gives him and their listeners an interesting answer. It's not enough to focus only on the law's first commandment.

Jesus quotes from Deuteronomy 6:4–5 and then from Leviticus 19:18. Jesus says the greatest commandments are those that command us to love God with all of our *heart* (the Middle Eastern mind), with all of our *soul* (the Middle Eastern animated body), and with all of our *strength* (what the Middle Eastern mind and body working in concert produce: good works). And then we are to love our neighbor as we love ourselves. Jesus is blunt that "there is no other commandment greater than these."

Our scribe is impressed. He states publicly that he agrees with Jesus. He reminds those listening to the exchange that keeping these two commandments is more important than all the burnt offerings and sacrifices made on temple altars. Recall that Jesus had just shamed the Sadducees in charge of that same sacrificial system. Others had been silenced, but this man is "not far from the kingdom of God."

Meditatio

The scribe asks Jesus, "Which is the first of all the commandments?" How would you answer the question? For me, a candidate for greatest commandment would be Exodus 20:12, to love and honor your parents so that your days might be long in the land. I feel that if we can get this commandment right then others will fall into place. When we honor our parents, we honor the family they built, and the family is the basic building block of culture in a godly society. Also, this is the only commandment that is followed by a promise, that we will live a long time in the land.

Do you see how each answer leaves us open to the possibility of further conversation? That is a way we grow in our understanding of our faith. Questions, good leading questions like the one asked by the scribe that day, will always lead us to deeper appreciation of our faith. Use this question in your meditation this week. Try a few others. See how the Spirit speaks to your heart in your answers.

Oratio

This prayer is known as "An Act of Love" and is a perfect response to the Gospel this week: *O my God, I love you above all things, with my whole heart and soul, because you are all-good and worthy of all my love. I love my neighbor as myself for the love or you. I forgive those who have injured me, and I ask pardon of all whom I have injured. Amen.*

Contemplatio

In the Bible we are called to love God with our whole heart, with our whole soul, and with all our strength. The biblical concept of "love" is perhaps best translated by the English concept of "attachment." We are called to be "attached" to God and to one another. The antonym of love is hate. If we are living in biblical love when we are attached to God and each other, then biblical hate must include being detached from God and others.

Love is a decision that we make to stay attached to another person, to a faith community, to the Lord. What steps are you willing to take this week to strengthen your attachment to God and others? Do we have any decisions to make? What events have we neglected? Small groups that we no longer attend? Home-bound elders we have not visited? That church service that somehow slips our mind and our schedule Sunday after Sunday? Make a decision to love this week. Make a decision to stay attached to God and to others in your community of faith. Pray that God will remind you of the ways that you can deepen your attachment to the Lord and each another.

OTHER READINGS: DEUTERONOMY 6:2–6; HEBREWS 7:23–28

THIRTY-SECOND SUNDAY IN ORDINARY TIME

BEWARE OF THE SCRIBES

MARK 12:38–44

38 In the course of his teaching he said, "Beware of the scribes, who like
to go around in long robes and accept greetings in the marketplaces,
39 seats of honor in synagogues, and places of honor at banquets. 40 They
devour the houses of widows and, as a pretext, recite lengthy prayers.
They will receive a very severe condemnation."

41 He sat down opposite the treasury and observed how the crowd put
money into the treasury. Many rich people put in large sums. 42 A poor
widow also came and put in two small coins worth a few cents. 43 Calling his disciples to himself, he said to them, "Amen, I say to you, this
poor widow put in more than all the other contributors to the treasury.
44 For they have all contributed from their surplus wealth, but she, from
her poverty, has contributed all she had, her whole livelihood."

Lectio

Jesus met a sympathetic scribe in the Gospel reading last week and told him that he was not far from the kingdom of God. It seems this particular scribe was exceptional, for this week Jesus launches into a denunciation of the whole class of scribes, those legal scholars who commanded respect for their ability to read and interpret the law of God for the Jewish community.

Jesus is teaching and people-watching on the temple mount. Groups of scribes are passing through. "Beware of the scribes," he warns his disciples. He unveils the true character of these religious leaders, who do everything they can to seek public praise. Jesus notices how they walk around wearing long, flowing robes that draw attention to themselves. This is a reference to the "elongated tassels" he mentions in Matthew 23:5. Like every other Jewish man, Jesus himself wore a prayer shawl with tassels at its four corners. It was a common belief that when Messiah appeared the tassels of his robe would bring healing to those who grasped them in faith (see Matthew 9:20). These scribes, Jesus suggests, imagine themselves to be the Messiah! Flowing robes and extra-long tassels are crowd-pleasers.

The scribes also love to be greeted in the marketplace. According to Jewish custom recorded in the Talmud, when two men meet in the marketplace the one with an inferior knowledge of the law should greet the other first. This is why the scribes wait so anxiously to be greeted. They crave the honor associated with this public exchange. Similarly, the "seats of honor in synagogues" were those that faced the congregation and that provided a backrest on the same wall as the scroll tabernacle. The "places of honor at banquets" are the seats to the immediate right and left of the host, where a scribe would be seen by all who enter the room.

Behind such overtly pious public displays, these scribes had actually exploited the most vulnerable people in the community. They had contrived ways to "devour the houses of widows," an offense worthy of divine condemnation. Jesus is fed up with this parade of fools. He takes a seat near the entrance to the temple court and watches as the faithful make their contributions to the treasury. These offerings would be divided three ways—for general temple upkeep, for the support of the Levitical priests and their families, and for the fund supporting widows and orphans. Jesus praises the large donations made by the wealthy. He can hear the sounds ringing as handfuls of coins clatter through the opening and into the stone collection vessels. This is as it should be. God blessed you, and you return an offering to God in thanksgiving.

Then Jesus notices a "poor widow" entering the temple area. He is shocked as he watches her make an offering well beyond her means. She is contributing to a collection that is supposed to support her as a widow. We sometimes read this passage as Jesus commending the widow for her devotion. But in context, it seems that Jesus is not pleased. He is angry, and his response to her contribution is a lament. Who taught this poor widow to make such an offering: everything she had to live on? Jesus realizes that the scribes had encouraged this behavior—this is how they could "devour the houses of widows." It is a living lesson for his disciples. The widow is following the teaching of the religious leaders but they have misled her, while she is risking everything to honor their teaching.

It is the last straw. Jesus leaves the temple mount and does not speak again until he predicts the destruction of this temple from a vantage point across the Kidron Valley, halfway up the Mount of Olives.

How important is it to you how you appear to others? What is the modern equivalent of dressing to stand out, of loving to be greeted in the marketplace and having the best seats in church and at a special meal? Would you pray a longer prayer for the sake of appearances? If we are men and women who love the Lord, we should comport ourselves among the community of faith, in our families, among our friends and neighbors, in a way that brings honor to the Lord and others before it brings honor to ourselves.

Jesus demonstrates what it means to be a leader when, in the middle of the Last Supper Passover liturgy, he leaves his position as host and systematically washes the feet of his disciples seated around the table. The gesture is dramatic. He comes last to Peter, who had the seat of highest honor on the right side of Jesus, and Peter at first tries to refuse this gesture of love.

Take a few moments this week to meditate on what being a leader like this would look like in your church, in your family, and among your friends and neighbors. Pray that the Lord will show you where you can serve, without thought of honor or reward. Be open to the opportunities the Spirit will provide in your ongoing training this week.

Oratio

Jesus challenges his disciples to avoid the abuses of the scribes. One such abuse was the recitation of long prayers for the sake of appearance. This week we can counter that temptation with a simple and direct prayer, the Jesus Prayer from the Orthodox Church. Pray it this week. Commit it to memory. Lean into it in times of need. It is a way for a believer to follow the instruction of St. Paul to "pray always and never lose heart." *"Lord Jesus Christ, Son of the living God, have mercy on me, a sinner."* Amen.

Contemplatio

Widows and orphans. They hold a special place in the heart of God and in the Bible they are commended to our special care and concern. This might be a good week to seek out and bless a widow or an orphan. Each week I reach out to "Ms. Laura." She is the "poor widow" that the Lord put in my life, and she has brought me so much joy by allowing me to serve her for the past eighteen years. It is never easy, rarely convenient, but always rewarding to greet her, to serve her, and to honor her in any way that I can. Ask the Lord to show you your own Ms. Laura and then find a way to bless that person. You will know the joy of the Lord through your efforts and delight the heart of our Father at the same time.

OTHER READINGS: 1 KINGS 17:10–16; HEBREWS 9:24–28

THIRTY-THIRD SUNDAY IN ORDINARY TIME

A LESSON FROM THE FIG TREE

MARK 13:24–32

24 "But in those days after that tribulation
the sun will be darkened,
and the moon will not give its light,
25 and the stars will be falling from the sky,
and the powers in the heavens will be shaken.

26 And then they will see 'the Son of Man coming in the clouds' with
great power and glory, 27 and then he will send out the angels and
gather [his] elect from the four winds, from the end of the earth to the
end of the sky.

28 "Learn a lesson from the fig tree. When its branch becomes tender
and sprouts leaves, you know that summer is near. 29 In the same way,
when you see these things happening, know that he is near, at the gates.
30 Amen, I say to you, this generation will not pass away until all these
things have taken place. 31 Heaven and earth will pass away, but my
words will not pass away.

32 "But of that day or hour, no one knows, neither the angels in heaven,
nor the Son, but only the Father."

Lectio

"But in those days after that tribulation …" This is a dramatic opening to the Gospel. We enter the narrative mid-stream and will need more context to appreciate this teaching of Jesus. In the thirteenth chapter in the Gospel of Mark, Jesus predicts the temple's destruction. He tells the apostles that not a single one of its stones will be left upon another. Andrew, Peter, James, and John then ask Jesus a two-part question. When will the temple be destroyed? Will the end of the world soon follow? Jesus will answer the first of these two questions but not the second. Jesus confidently predicts that the destruction of the temple will occur within the next forty years—a biblical generation (verse 30). Anyone who heard him speak these words could live long enough to see them fulfilled in their own lifetime. And indeed, the temple is destroyed by Roman armies under the command of General Titus in 70 AD.

Jesus draws a literary allusion to help them understand the days of tribulation that will lead up to the temple's demise. He quotes the prophet Isaiah's words (Isaiah 13:10, 34:4) predicting the times culminating in the Assyrian onslaught that destroyed the northern kingdom of ancient Israel in 721 BC. The Assyrian army was so vast, so violently bent on destruction, that its arrival seemed to darken the sun. Entire empires fell in quick succession like stars falling from the skies as the Assyrians advanced from the north. The devastation of these armies was so complete it seemed like the "powers in the heavens" were shaken. The ten tribes of the northern kingdom were driven into an exile from which they never returned.

Isaiah put his prophetic reputation on the line and his words were fulfilled. Jesus attaches these same words to his pronouncement against the temple, the symbol of Jewish national identity. When the Roman armies besiege Jerusalem and dismantle the temple people will remember his prophetic word. Jesus will then be recognized as the divine figure of Daniel's vision—the "Son of Man" and Messiah who made this bold prediction of destruction so clear to his followers. Jesus will be vindicated as these events work themselves out within the next forty years of Israel's history.

Jesus refuses to answer the second part of the apostles' question. If the temple is to be destroyed, then when will the final judgment be revealed? About that day, that time, that hour he will not speak. He counsels his followers to remain alert and watchful. All they can know is that with the dismantling of the temple the clock will begin ticking toward the end.

Meditatio

What do fig trees and predictions about the destruction of the temple have to do with each other? Jesus teaches that we should learn a lesson from the fig tree. It will help us in our meditation this week to know that fig trees in Galilee were known to produce a new crop as many as four times annually. Anyone anxious to sample the fruit would pay constant attention to leaves and buds. If the branches are tender and sprouts of fruit appear then you know the harvest is close. You check the tree daily in anticipation of ripe figs. Jesus wants his disciples to read the signs of the times in the same way. Be awake, be alert, be watchful so that you will know when you are to "flee to the mountains" (Mark 13:14) in advance of the arrival of Roman armies coming on the scene of history to lay siege to the holy city.

We might not have fig trees in our yards to assist us in our careful examination (I do, but that is another story) but we can take the lesson of the fig tree to heart. We can be open to the gentle promptings of the Spirit that tell us that the branches of our life are becoming tender and its fruit is beginning to bud. We can be careful to tend and care for these gentle nudges of God as we seek to live in the will of the Lord and find new opportunities to serve others. Take a few moments this week to do a "branch check" and see what season of life you are in, and what season in life approaches. Are the branches of your life tender? Is there the promise of fruit in the future? Is some pruning going to be needed to increase the harvest? These are all good questions to ask in our meditation this week.

Oratio

The penultimate verse of the Book of Revelation responds to another prediction of Jesus. It is a perfect prayer this week. Jesus has revealed to the apostle John that his testimony is true and assures the apostle that yes, he is coming soon. We can join together with the apostle in his heartfelt prayer: *"Amen [Yes]! Come, Lord Jesus!"*

Contemplatio

Why are we obsessed with knowing the future? The disciples want to know the day, the time, and the hour of the final judgment. Jesus refuses to answer their question because he knows that doing so would not benefit them in any way, shape, or form.

Concerned Christians have been trying to predict the day, the time, and the hour of the end of the world for thousands of years. The one thing common among such predictions is that they have all been wrong! I'm convinced that if Christians knew the exact day and time of the end of the world and the final judgment that most (myself included, I am afraid) might live like sinners right up to the day before! The counsel of Jesus is simple. Be awake and alert. Be watchful in anticipation, reading the signs of the times.

I am reminded that the late Dr. Billy Graham taught that fascination with knowing the date of the end times was futile since the only "end time" that you have anything to say about is your own! He pleaded with those who listened to get right with the Lord while you are on this side of the grave. Your personal end time will come soon enough. He wanted you to be ready when it does. I like that advice. It gives me hope for the present.

When I was a graduate student at Fuller Theological Seminary in Pasadena a professor had a clever bumper sticker on his car: "Jesus is coming! Look busy!" I will never forget that message, and I hope it might inspire you as well. We know that the Lord will return one day. Until then let us remain busy loving and serving others in his name.

OTHER READINGS: DANIEL 12:1–3; HEBREWS 10:11–14, 18

OUR LORD JESUS CHRIST, KING OF THE UNIVERSE

YOU ARE A KING?

JOHN 18:33–37

> 33 So Pilate went back into the praetorium and summoned Jesus and
> said to him, "Are you the King of the Jews?" 34 Jesus answered, "Do
> you say this on your own or have others told you about me?" 35 Pilate
> answered, "I am not a Jew, am I? Your own nation and the chief priests
> handed you over to me. What have you done?" 36 Jesus answered, "My
> kingdom does not belong to this world. If my kingdom did belong to
> this world, my attendants [would] be fighting to keep me from being
> handed over to the Jews. But as it is, my kingdom is not here." 37 So
> Pilate said to him, "Then you are a king?" Jesus answered, "You say I am
> a king. For this I was born and for this I came into the world, to testify
> to the truth. Everyone who belongs to the truth listens to my voice."

This weekend the liturgical year comes to an end as the faithful gather to celebrate the feast called "Christ the King." It is telling that our reading is from the passion narrative in John's Gospel. Jesus is engaged in a forced conversation with the Roman governor about accusations that Jesus is claiming to be a king like Caesar in Rome. I will also focus attention on Daniel 7, the first reading in this week's liturgy. This important text from the prophet Daniel provides insight into the role of Messiah as a divine figure who will rule as king in the name of the Ancient of Days.

At Jesus's arraignment, Pontius Pilate realizes that he is getting nowhere. The assembled religious leaders are determined to have Jesus sentenced to death. Pilate summons Jesus into the praetorium, his private residence, where he asks Jesus directly if he claims to be "the King of the Jews." Jesus evades the confrontational aspect of the inquiry and turns the tables back on Pilate with a question of his own. Why do you want to know? Is your interest in my answer genuine, or are you questioning me at the bidding of the religious officials who brought me before you today?

Pilate's response is unique. "I am not a Jew, am I?" He admits to Jesus that he does not understand why the chief priests are so threatened by Jesus nor why they want him sentenced to death. Pilate needs to know more. He asks Jesus to state in his own words just what he has done to raise their ire. The issue of kingship is raised in response to this question. Jesus indirectly admits that he is in fact a king—but of a kingdom that does not belong to this world. The difference, he assures Pilate, is that subjects of an earthly king would have fought for him. They would have resisted the efforts of the religious authorities to take him into custody. And yet here he is, standing before the representative of Rome's empire. Pilate knows there have been no riots, no violent actions attributed to Jesus and his band of followers to date.

Pilate is confused. Perhaps understandably at a loss, he asks, "Then you are a king?" He does not know what Jesus is claiming. What is this otherworldly kingdom, and where is it to be found in the empire? These questions direct our attention to our reading from Daniel. The prophet receives a heavenly vision where a male figure rides the clouds into the throne room of heaven. This "one like a son of man" is presented before God, the heavenly judge, the Ancient of Days. Daniel senses the royal bearing of this figure and watches and records as the "son of man" is given all the benefits of an earthly king, with an additional promise that his royal throne will never be destroyed. His rule will last forever. This vision is the source of the title that Jesus uses frequently of himself. He is telling his followers that he is a divine agent sent by God to claim a throne that will last beyond the end of time. He is in fact a king—but of a kind Pilate knows nothing about.

Meditatio

Jesus informs Pilate that his kingdom does not belong to this world. Elsewhere, Jesus calls it the "kingdom of God." That kingdom has been breaking forth all over Israel as a result of Jesus's public ministry. This eternal kingdom is different from all other kingdoms that have come before. Its king has ridden a lowly female donkey, with a young colt trailing behind, down the slopes of the Mount of Olives before entering the holy city. This gesture fulfilled a centuries-old prophecy (Zechariah 9:9). There would be no royal chariot for King Jesus. In his kingdom rulers will not "lord it over" subjects but will serve them. And King Jesus has demonstrated what his kind of leadership means at the last supper when he wrapped a towel around his waist and washed the feet of each of the apostles. "I have given you a model to follow, so that as I have done for you, you should also do" (John 13:15).

It is part of our national identity as Americans to resist the rule of tyrant kings. Our first President rejected the opportunity to become a king. Our founders knew the perils associated with kings and kingdoms. They wanted no part of kings, present or future. But Jesus is a different kind of king. He is our King, our Lord and Savior, but also our brother and friend. He reminds us in word and deed that he came to serve rather than to be served. He came to lay down his life for the ransom of the many. Take these thoughts to heart as you meditate.

Oratio

Let's pray with King David in Psalm 24:7–10: "Lift up your heads, O gates; be lifted you ancient portals, that the king of glory may enter. Who is this king of glory? The LORD, strong and mighty, the LORD, mighty in war. Lift up your heads, O gates; rise up you ancient portals that the king of glory may enter. Who is this king of glory? The LORD of hosts, he is the king of glory."

Contemplatio

Jesus tells Pilate that he was born to testify to the truth. This is why he came into the world. Why were you born? Why did you come into the world? When I was young, children in the Catholic community were taught the basics of the faith through the questions and answers of the Baltimore Catechism. I will always remember the first set of questions. They included, "Why did God make you?" The answer is simple, direct, and powerful. All persons are created to know, to love, and to serve the Lord—and to be happy with him in heaven. That was the answer we were to commit to memory.

How can we advance in each of the areas listed above? What would it look like to know, love, and serve the Lord more this week? If we want to know the Lord better we need to dedicate time in our schedule to study the Lord in the Word. Recommit yourself to daily Bible reading and to ongoing Bible study. If we want to love the Lord more this week we can embrace the biblical notion of love as attachment and get ourselves reattached to a community of believers who can help us grow. If we are to serve the Lord more effectively we need to find ways to put our faith into action. We need to show up and assist others less fortunate than ourselves. These are three goals worth committing to memory and acting upon this week. They will also give us a head start on enjoying God and being happy with him. Godspeed!

OTHER READINGS: DANIEL 7:13–14; REVELATION 1:5–8

MORE RESOURCES

ABOUT THE AUTHOR

Kevin Saunders is a Catholic Bible teacher in Phoenix, Arizona. He became particularly interested in the cultural world of Jesus while living in the Old City of Jerusalem. His popular Bible class can be found online at ArizonaBibleClass.com.

CATHOLIC MINISTRIES

For more on the practice of Lectio Divina, we recommend the book *Pray with the Bible, Meditate with the Word* (ABS Item 122590V), available on Bibles.com in English and Spanish.

American Bible Society's Catholic Initiatives offers resources in digital, video, and print formats. Visit us at catholic.americanbible.org.

www.ingramcontent.com/pod-product-compliance
Lightning Source LLC
LaVergne TN
LVHW050640100826
845148LV00011B/1918

* 9 7 8 1 5 8 5 1 6 4 2 8 8 *